Essential Chinese

Edited by
Erin Quirk and Tanying Dong

 LIVING LANGUAGE®

Content in this program has been modified and enhanced from *Starting Out in Chinese*, published in 2008.

Published in the United States by Living Language, an imprint of Random House, Inc.

www.livinglanguage.com

Editor: Erin Quirk
Production Editor: Ciara Robinson
Production Manager: Tom Marshall
Interior Design: Sophie Chin
Illustrations: Sophie Chin

First Edition

Library of Congress Cataloging-in-Publication Data

Essential Chinese / edited by Erin Quirk and Tanying Dong. — 1st ed.
p. cm.
ISBN 978-0-307-97165-4
1. Chinese language—Textbooks for foreign speakers—English. 2. Chinese language—Grammar.
3. Chinese language—Spoken Chinese. I. Quirk, Erin. II. Dong, Tanying.
PL1129.E5.E884 2011
495.1'82421—dc23

                                    2011021870

PRINTED IN THE UNITED STATES OF AMERICA

10 9 8 7 6

Acknowledgments

Thanks to the Living Language team: Amanda D'Acierno, Christopher Warnasch, Suzanne McQuade, Laura Riggio, Erin Quirk, Amanda Munoz, Fabrizio LaRocca, Siobhan O'Hare, Sophie Chin, Sue Daulton, Alison Skrabek, Carolyn Roth, Ciara Robinson, and Tom Marshall.

How to Use This Course **6**

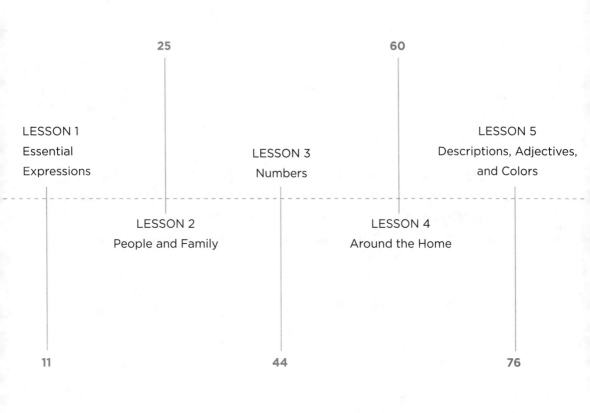

COURSE

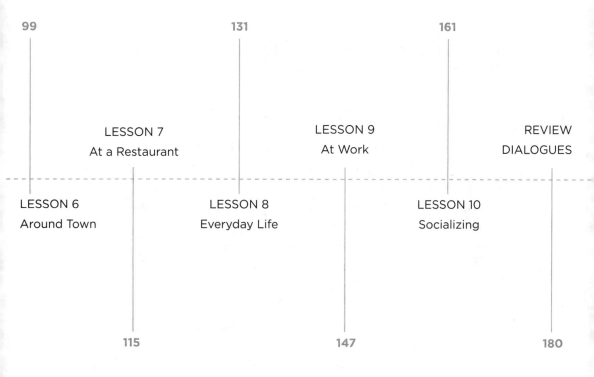
OUTLINE

How to Use This Course

Nǐ hǎo. 你好。

Welcome to *Living Language Essential Chinese*! Ready to learn how to speak, read, and write Chinese?

Before we begin, let's go over what you'll see in this course. It's very easy to use, but this section will help you get started.

PINYIN AND CHARACTERS

This course includes both Chinese characters and pīnyīn, the phonetic system used to represent Chinese pronunciation. Pīnyīn is mostly straightforward: p sounds like the *p* in *place*, and y sounds like the *y* in *yes*. But there are some spellings that you'll need to get used to, and there are special diacritics to represent tones. You don't need to do anything extra to prepare to read pīnyīn; it will come naturally as you progress through the course and listen to the audio. But if you'd like an overview of pīnyīn and Chinese pronunciation, you can refer to the *Pronunciation and Pīnyīn Guide* at the back of this book.

Chinese characters are a bit more difficult to master! Through *Essential Chinese*, you'll see Take It Further sections that focus on a handful of important characters from the lesson you're working on. These sections are meant to be recognition exercises; don't try to write out the characters at first. As you progress through the lessons, you'll learn to recognize more and more characters, building up to a character vocabulary of over 100 essential words and phrases. You'll complete review practices that recycle characters from previous lessons, and soon enough, you'll be able to read phrases and even sentences.

This course also comes with the *Guide to Chinese Characters*, which is a step-by-step introduction to reading and writing Chinese characters. You'll be directed to certain lessons in the guide as you progress through this course, so you'll be working with both *Essential Chinese* and the *Guide to Chinese Characters* simultaneously. This way you'll learn how to recognize important characters, and eventually you'll learn clues that will help you decipher character meanings, as well as things like types of strokes and stroke order that will help you write the characters you learn.

LESSONS

There are 10 lessons in this course. Each lesson is divided into three parts and has the following components:

Welcome at the beginning, outlining what you will cover in each of the three parts of the lesson.

PART 1

- **Vocabulary Builder 1** listing the key words and phrases for that lesson.

- **Vocabulary Practice 1** to practice what you learned in Vocabulary Builder 1.

- **Grammar Builder 1** to guide you through the structure of the Chinese language (how to form sentences, questions, and so on).

PART 2

- **Vocabulary Builder 2** listing more key words and phrases.

- **Vocabulary Practice 2** to practice what you learned in Vocabulary Builder 2.

- **Grammar Builder 2** for more information on language structure.

- **Work Out 1** for a comprehensive practice of what you've learned so far.

PART 3

- **Bring It All Together** to put what you've learned in a conversational context through a dialogue, monologue, description, or other similar text.

- **Work Out 2** for another helpful practice exercise, including additional audio-only practice on your audio.

- **Drive It Home** to ingrain an important point of Chinese structure for the long term.

- **Parting Words** outlining what you learned in the lesson.

TAKE IT FURTHER

There are two **Take It Further** sections in each lesson, after each Vocabulary Practice. As you read above, these sections will focus on important Chinese characters, helping you learn to recognize characters and read basic phrases and sentences. These sections will also refer you to particular lessons in your *Guide to Chinese Characters*, for further practice reading and writing Chinese.

WORD RECALL

Word Recall sections appear in between lessons. They review important vocabulary and grammar from previous lessons, including the one you just finished. These sections will reinforce what you've learned so far in the course, and help you retain the information for the long term.

QUIZZES

This course contains two quizzes: **Quiz 1** is halfway through the course (after Lesson 5), and **Quiz 2** appears after the last lesson (Lesson 10). The quizzes are self-graded so it's easy for you to test your progress and see if you should go back and review.

REVIEW DIALOGUES

There are five **Review Dialogues** at the end of the course, after Quiz 2. These everyday dialogues review what you learned in Lessons 1-10, introduce some new vocabulary and structures, and allow you to become more familiar with conversational Chinese. Each dialogue is followed by comprehension questions that serve as the course's final review.

PROGRESS BAR

You will see a **Progress Bar** on almost every page that has course material. It indicates your current position in the course and lets you know how much progress you're making. Each line in the bar represents a lesson, with the final line representing the Review Dialogues.

AUDIO

Look for this symbol ⊙ to help guide you through the audio as you're reading the book. It will tell you which track to listen to for each section that has audio. When you see the symbol, select the indicated track and start listening! If you don't see the symbol, then there isn't any audio for that section. You'll also see ⒨, which will tell you where that track ends.

The audio can be used on its own—in other words, without the book—when you're on the go. Whether in your car or at the gym, you can listen to the audio to brush up on your pronunciation or review what you've learned in the book.

PRONUNCIATION AND PINYIN GUIDE, GRAMMAR SUMMARY, GLOSSARY

At the back of this book you will find a **Pronunciation and Pīnyīn Guide**, **Grammar Summary**, and **Glossary**. The Pronunciation and Pīnyīn Guide provides information on Chinese pronunciation and the pīnyīn phonetic system used in this course. The Grammar Summary contains a helpful, brief overview of key points in the Chinese grammar system. The Glossary (Chinese-English and English-Chinese) includes all of the essential words from the ten lessons, as well as additional key vocabulary. It is arranged alphabetically by pīnyīn, but characters are included as well.

FREE ONLINE TOOLS

Go to **www.livinglanguage.com/languagelab** to access your free online tools. The tools are organized around the lessons in this course, with audiovisual flashcards and interactive games and quizzes. These tools will help you review and practice the vocabulary and grammar that you've seen in the lessons, as well provide some extra words and phrases related to the lesson's topic.

Lesson 1: Essential Expressions

Dì-yī kè: Jīběn yòngyǔ

第一课: 基本用语

Hello. Nǐ hǎo. 你好。 In this lesson, you'll kick off your Chinese learning adventure by becoming familiar with the pronunciation and different tones used in Chinese, and you'll learn some basic expressions to get you started speaking right away. You'll learn how to:

☐ Say *hello* and ask how someone is doing.

☐ Distinguish among the four tones in Mandarin.

☐ Say *thank you* and use other common courtesy expressions.

☐ Learn how to politely get someone's attention.

☐ Put it all together in a few simple exchanges.

So let's get started with some simple greetings. Ready?

Remember to look for this symbol ⊙ to help guide you through the audio when you're reading the book. It will tell you which track to listen to for each section that has audio. When you see the symbol, select the indicated track and start listening. If you don't see the symbol, there isn't any audio for the section. You'll also see ⊙, which will tell you where the track ends. Finally, keep in mind that the audio can be used on its own for review and practice on the go!

Vocabulary Builder 1

1B Vocabulary Builder 1 (CD 1, Track 2)

good, fine	hǎo	好
you	nǐ	你
Hello.	Nǐ hǎo.	你好。
How are you?	Nǐ hǎo ma?	你好吗？
I	wǒ	我
very well	hěn hǎo	很好
I'm fine.	Wǒ hěn hǎo.	我很好。
And you?	Nǐ ne?	你呢？
Not bad.	Bùcuò.	不错 。

Vocabulary Practice 1

Now let's practice what you've learned. Match the English in the left column to the Chinese equivalent in the right.

1. I	a. hǎo 好
2. Hello.	b. Wǒ hěn hǎo. 我很好。
3. good, fine	c. wǒ 我
4. you	d. Bùcuò. 不错。
5. I'm fine.	e. Nǐ hǎo. 你好。
6. Not bad.	f. nǐ 你

ANSWER KEY

1. c; 2. e; 3. a; 4. f; 5. b; 6. d

Take It Further 1

The most difficult part of learning Chinese is probably learning the characters. As you can see, this course includes both pinyin, or rather pīnyīn, the Chinese transliteration alphabet, and characters, so you'll be able to gradually learn to recognize and write the characters.

This program comes with the *Guide to Chinese Characters*, which is an excellent resource for learning how to read and write in Chinese. You can work with the *Guide to Chinese Characters* simultaneously with this course book to master reading and writing while you're also learning to speak. You'll be reminded to turn to certain lessons in the guide after each Take It Further 1. But if you prefer, you can work your way through the *Guide to Chinese Characters* all at once at the beginning.

To help you recognize important characters from each lesson, we'll spend some time in these Take It Further sections with exercises on particular characters. These exercises are only meant to help you recognize certain characters. Don't try to write the characters just yet, because you'll need to learn important concepts like types of strokes and stroke order first. You'll find that, along with more comprehensive information on reading and writing Chinese characters, in the character guide.

Let's start with three common characters. Take a look at each one, and practice saying it aloud. If you can think of any mnemonic devices to help you, go right ahead. That's the best way to learn characters, especially in the beginning. We'll suggest a few for you in the first several lessons. For example, nǐ 你 is pronounced similarly to knee, and there are lines that look a bit like legs. Hǎo 好 is pronounced like how, and you might see something that looks like a question mark on the right hand side. Of course, these are just suggestions. If they don't work for you, come up with ones that make more sense to you!

你	nǐ	*you*
好	hǎo	*good, fine*
吗	ma	*a question particle*

Are you familiar with these three? See if you can remember them. Write out the pīnyīn for each one:

1. 好 _____

2. 吗 _____

3. 你 _____

ANSWER KEY
1. hǎo; 2. ma; 3. nǐ

Now, let's put them together in expressions you've already seen. Write out the pīnyīn for each of the following. Do you remember what they mean?

1. 你好。 _____

2. 你好吗? _____

ANSWER KEY
1. Nǐ hǎo. (*Hello.*) 2. Nǐ hǎo ma? (*How are you?*)

You'll learn Chinese characters gradually as you progress through this course. For a general introduction and some basic information, read the introduction and Lesson 1: Basic Strokes in your *Guide to Chinese Characters*.

Grammar Builder 1

▶ 1C Grammar Builder 1 (CD 1, Track 3)

Let's pause for a brief note regarding Nǐ hǎo 你好 and Nǐ hǎo ma? 你好吗? The exchange of Nǐ hǎo 你好 is very brief, just like saying *Hi*. Nǐ hǎo ma? 你好吗? is a question and most likely will prompt the answer Wǒ hěn hǎo 我很好 (*I'm fine*) or Bùcuò 不错 (*Not bad*), followed by Nǐ ne? 你呢? (*And you?*).

Before we move on, you may have noticed that these phrases have a bit of a sing-song quality to them. This is because Mandarin Chinese is a tonal language, causing the ups and downs you hear on the vowels. There are four tones in Mandarin Chinese, and each word has its designated tone or carries what is called a neutral tone.

First Tone	mā 妈	mother	This is a high-pitched tone that remains on the same pitch.
Second Tone	má 麻	hemp	This is a rising tone, from medium pitched to high.
Third Tone	mǎ 马	horse	This is a scooping tone, from low pitch to medium.
Fourth Tone	mà 骂	scold	This is a falling tone, very much like the stress that people put on their yes and no when they really mean it.
Neutral Tone	ma 吗	question particle	This is very much a resigned tone. Medium pitched and laid back, it usually appears at the end of a phrase.

Let's listen to all five tones together: mā, má, mǎ, mà, ma (妈, 麻, 马, 骂, 吗).

Beautiful. You'll put all the tones in the right places after you learn some words. Just remember to listen for them; they're a very essential part of speaking and understanding Chinese!

Vocabulary Builder 2

1D Vocabulary Builder 2 (CD 1, Track 4)

Thanks.	Xièxie.	谢谢。
You're welcome.	Bù kèqì.	不客气。
Excuse me. I'm sorry.	Duìbùqǐ.	对不起。
It's nothing. (Don't worry. No problem.)	Méi shì.	没事。
Goodbye.	Zàijiàn.	再见。

✎ Vocabulary Practice 2

Fill in the missing pīnyīn syllables in each of the following phrases. Don't forget to add the tone marks. A syllable can mean different things depending on the tone it carries!

1. Duìbù _____. (*Excuse me.*)

2. _____ xie. (*Thanks.*)

3. Zài _____. (*Goodbye.*)

4. Bù _____ qì. (*You're welcome.*)

5. _____ shì. (*It's nothing.*)

ANSWER KEY

1. qī; 2. Xiè; 3. jiàn; 4. kè; 5. Méi

Take It Further 2

Let's take a closer look at a few more essential characters from this lesson. Study these characters, and try to think of any devices that will help you remember them.

我	wǒ	*I*
很	hěn	*very*
谢	xiè	*thank*

Are you familiar with these three? Let's review them, and bring back the other characters we focused on. Match the Chinese on the left with the pīnyīn and English on the right.

1. 很	a. wǒ (*I*)
2. 你	b. hǎo (*good, fine*)
3. 好	c. ma (*question particle*)
4. 我	d. hěn (*very*)
5. 谢	e. nǐ (*you*)
6. 吗	f. xiè (*thank*)

ANSWER KEY

1. d; 2. e; 3. b; 4. a; 5. f; 6. c

Now, try to give the pīnyīn and meanings of these sentences.

1. 很好。 _____

2. 我很好。 _____

3. 谢谢。 _____

ANSWER KEY

1. Hěn hǎo. (*Very good.*) 2. Wǒ hěn hǎo. (*I'm fine.*) 3. Xièxie. (*Thanks.*)

Grammar Builder 2

▶ 1E Grammar Builder 2 (CD 1, Track 5)

When apologizing, you can use Duìbùqǐ 对不起 (*I am sorry*) for any occasion. After you get someone's attention, you can go on to explain exactly what you need if you have to with one of the following expressions.

Let me go by.	Qǐng ràng yī xià?	请让一下？
May I trouble you?	Dǎrǎo yī xià?	打扰一下？
May I ask you a question?	Qǐngwèn yī xià?	请问一下？

Ⓘ

✎ Work Out 1

Let's practice saying hello and asking someone how they are with an audio comprehension exercise. Listen to the audio, and fill in the blanks with the missing words that you hear. Make sure you use the correct tone mark in the pīnyīn; listen carefully to the recordings to distinguish among them.

▶ 1F Work Out 1 (CD 1, Track 6)

1. *Hello.*

   Nǐ _____.

   你好。

2. *How are you?*

   _____ hǎo ma?

   你好吗？

3. *I'm fine.*

_____ hǎo.

我很好。

4. *And you?*

Nǐ _____ ?

你呢？

5. *Not bad.*

Bù_____ .

不错。

6. *Thanks.*

_____ .

谢谢。

7. *You're welcome.*

_____ .

不客气。

8. *Excuse me./I'm sorry.*

_____ .

对不起。

9. *It's nothing.*

_____ shì.

没事。

Lesson 1: Essential Expressions

10. *Goodbye.*

Zài _____.

再见。

ANSWER KEY

1. hǎo; 2. Nǐ; 3. Wǒ hěn; 4. ne; 5. cuò; 6. Xièxie; 7. Bù kèqi; 8. Duìbùqǐ; 9. Méi; 10. jiàn

Bring It All Together

▶ 1G Bring It All Together (CD 1, Track 7)

Let's bring it all together in a few brief dialogues. First you'll hear the English, then the Chinese. Be sure to repeat the Chinese in the pauses provided.

Zhāng:	Nǐ hǎo.
	你好。
	Hello.
Jìng:	Nǐ hǎo.
	你好。
	Hi.
Zhāng:	Nǐ hǎo ma?
	你好吗?
	How are you?
Jìng:	Wǒ hěn hǎo, nǐ ne?
	我很好, 你呢?
	I'm fine, and you?
Zhāng:	Bùcuò.
	不错。
	Not bad.

Let's listen to another brief exchange.

Zhāng:	Duìbùqǐ.
	对不起。
	I am sorry.
Jìng:	Méi shì.
	没事。
	It's nothing.
Zhāng:	Xièxie.
	谢谢。
	Thanks.
Jìng:	Bù kèqì.
	不客气。
	You're welcome.
Zhāng:	Zàijiàn.
	再见。
	Goodbye.

✎ Work Out 2

Let's look at a dialogue you're familiar with. Fill in the missing pīnyīn, using the English translations as a guide. If the Chinese characters help you, that's fantastic!

1. *I am sorry.*

   _____ bùqǐ.

   对不起。

2. *It's nothing.*

   Méi _____.

   没事。

3. *Thanks.*

   Xiè _____.

   谢谢。

4. *You're welcome.*

   _____ kèqì.

   不客气。

5. *Goodbye.*

   _____ jiàn.

   再见。

   ANSWER KEY
   1. Duì; 2. shì; 3. xie; 4. Bù; 5. Zài

▶ 1H Work Out 2 (CD 1, Track 8)

Now listen to your audio for some more audio-only practice. This will help tune your ear to Chinese, improve your pronunciation, and eventually help you become a stronger speaker.

⏸

✎ Drive It Home

Throughout this course you'll see Drive It Home sections that include practices on key constructions that you've learned. At first glance, these exercises may seem simple and repetitive, so you may be tempted to skip them. But don't! These exercises are designed to help make the structures that you learn more automatic, and to move them into your long-term memory. So take the time to do each exercise completely, writing out all the answers, and speaking them aloud to yourself. This will really help you retain the information.

Let's review some greetings. Read each line aloud, and then translate the answer in parentheses into pīnyīn.

1. Nǐ hǎo ma? 你好吗? *(Very well.)* _____

2. Nǐ hǎo ma? 你好吗? *(I'm fine.)* _____

3. Nǐ hǎo ma? 你好吗? *(Not bad.)* _____

4. Nǐ hǎo ma? 你好吗? *(Very well. And you?)* _____

ANSWER KEY
1. Hěn hǎo. 2. Wǒ hěn hǎo. 3. Bùcuò. 4. Hěn hǎo. Nǐ ne?

Parting Words

Very nice. Hěn hǎo. 很好。 You've made it through your first lesson of Chinese. *Congratulations!* Gōngxǐ nǐ! 恭喜你！By now you should be able to:

☐ Say *hello* and ask how someone is doing. (Still unsure? Go back to 12.)

☐ Distinguish among the four tones in Mandarin. (Still unsure? Go back to 15.)

☐ Say *thank you* and use other common courtesy expressions.
(Still unsure? Go back to 16.)

☐ Learn how to politely get someone's attention. (Still unsure? Go back to 18.)

☐ Put it all together in a few simple exchanges. (Still unsure? Go back to 20.)

Don't forget to practice and reinforce what you've learned by visiting **www.livinglanguage.com/languagelab** for flashcards, games, and quizzes for Lesson One!

Word Recall

You will see this section between each lesson. It gives you the chance to review key vocabulary from all of the previous lessons up to that point, not only the lesson you've just completed. This will reinforce the vocabulary, as well as some of the structures, that you've learned so far in the course, so that you can retain them in your long-term memory. For now, though, we'll only review the key vocabulary you learned in lesson 1. Match the English on the left with the Chinese (and pīnyīn) on the right.

1. *I*	a. Xièxie. 谢谢。
2. *you*	b. Nǐ hǎo. 你好。
3. *not bad*	c. Bù kèqì. 不客气。
4. *Thanks*	d. wǒ 我
5. *That's nothing.*	e. Zàijiàn. 再见。
6. *Hello.*	f. hǎo 好
7. *good, fine*	g. Nǐ ne? 你呢？
8. *I am sorry.*	h. Méi shì. 没事。
9. *very*	i. nǐ 你
10. *You're welcome.*	j. hěn 很
11. *And you?*	k. bùcuò 不错
12. *Goodbye.*	l. Duìbùqǐ. 对不起。

ANSWER KEY
1. d; 2. i; 3. k; 4. a; 5. h; 6. b; 7. f; 8. l; 9. j; 10. c; 11. g; 12. e

Lesson 2: People and Family

Dì-èr kè: Rén yǔ jiātíng

第二课: 人与家庭

Nǐ hǎo. 你好。*Hello.* Are you ready for your second lesson of Chinese? In this lesson you'll focus on:

☐ Basic vocabulary for talking about people.

☐ The verb *be* and the pronouns *I, you, he, she,* and so on.

☐ Key vocabulary related to the family.

☐ The verb *have.*

☐ A few short conversations about people and the family.

Vocabulary Builder 1

▶ 2B Vocabulary Builder 1 (CD 1, Track 11)

to be	shì	是
I, me	wǒ	我
you	nǐ	你
he, him	tā	他
she, her	tā	她
we, us	wǒmen	我们
you (plural)	nǐmen	你们
they, them	tāmen	他们
person, people	rén	人
female	nǚ	女
woman	nǚrén	女人
male	nán	男
man	nánrén	男人
teacher	lǎoshī	老师
student	xuésheng	学生

Ⅱ

✎ Vocabulary Practice 1

A. Let's practice some of those new words. Translate each pīnyīn word into English.

1. nǚrén _____

2. nǐmen _____

3. shì _____

4. nánrén _____

5. lǎoshī _____

B. Now translate the English word into pīnyīn.

1. *student* _____

2. *he, him* _____

3. *we, us* _____

4. *they, them* _____

5. *person, people* _____

ANSWER KEY
A. 1. *woman*; 2. *you (plural)*; 3. *to be*; 4. *man*; 5. *teacher*
B. 1. xuésheng; 2. tā; 3. wǒmen; 4. tāmen; 5. rén

Take It Further 1

Okay, let's focus on some important Chinese characters. In Lesson 1, we took a look at wǒ 我 (*I, me*) and nǐ 你 (*you*). Notice that these pronouns can be used as a subject (*I am . . . , you are . . .*) or as an object (*. . . me, . . . you*). The same is true of the other pronouns. Even though *he/him* and *she/her* are pronounced the same way, they have two different characters. Finally, notice that to make plural pronouns, you just add 们 -men to the singular forms. Study these characters for the pronouns you've just learned in this lesson.

他	tā	*he, him*
她	tā	*she, her*
我们	wǒmen	*we, us*
你们	nǐmen	*you (plural)*
他们	tāmen	*they, them*

Okay? Let's see if you can recognize them. We'll start with the singulars, including the ones you learned in Lesson 1, then move to plurals. Give the pīnyīn and translation for each.

1. 他 _____

2. 你 _____

3. 她 _____

4. 我 _____

5. 你们 _____

6. 我们 _____

7. 他们 _____

ANSWER KEY

1. tā (*he, him*); 2. nǐ (*you*); 3. tā (*she, her*); 4. wǒ (*I, me*); 5. nǐmen (*you, plural*); 6. wǒmen (*we, us*);
7. tāmen (*they, them*)

If you'd like to turn to your character guide, this is a good time to cover Lesson 2:
More Basic Strokes.

Grammar Builder 1

▶ 2C Grammar Builder 1 (CD 1, Track 12)

You just heard some pronouns, the little words used to indicate *I, you, he, she*, etc.
Let's look at them once more, as they're an important piece of the puzzle.

I, me	wǒ	我
you	nǐ	你
he, him	tā	他
she, her	tā	她
we, us	wǒmen	我们
you (plural)	nǐmen	你们
they, them	tāmen	他们

Now let's use those pronouns to build some phrases. In Chinese there is only one way of saying *is, are, was, were,* and *will be,* and that's using the verb shì 是, which means *to be.* The same form of this verb is used for every person, every thing, and for all times, past, present, and future.

The best news is that this rule applies to all Chinese verbs. No matter if you are talking about one person or five people, yourself or others, the past or the future, every verb has only one form, making it much easier to memorize. So, to say *I am, you are, he is,* etc., simply use the appropriate pronoun followed by the verb shì 是.

I am	wǒ shì	我是
you are	nǐ shì	你是
he is	tā shì	他是
she is	tā shì	她是
we are	wǒmen shì	我们是
you (plural) are	nǐmen shì	你们是
they are	tāmen shì	他们是

More good news: in Chinese, you don't use an article, such as *a, an,* or *the,* before a noun. Let's start to form some sentences using this pattern.

She is a woman.	Tā shì nǚrén.	她是女人。
He is a man.	Tā shì nánrén.	他是男人。
The teacher is a woman.	Lǎoshī shì nǚrén.	老师是女人。
The student is a man.	Xuésheng shì nánrén.	学生是男人。

Ⅱ

Vocabulary Builder 2

▶ 2D Vocabulary Builder 2 (CD 1, Track 13)

to have	yǒu	有
question word	ma	吗
Do you have ... ?	Nǐ yǒu ... ma?	你有 ... 吗?
older brother	gēge	哥哥
younger brother	dìdi	弟弟
older sister	jiějie	姐姐
younger sister	mèimei	妹妹
son	érzi	儿子
daughter	nǚ'ér	女儿
father	fùqin	父亲
mother	mǔqīn	母亲

⏸

✎ Vocabulary Practice 2

Let's review family vocabulary. Fill in the following family tree with the correct Chinese word for each member of the family. For this exercise, you're the youngest of three, so use the terms for older brother and older sister.

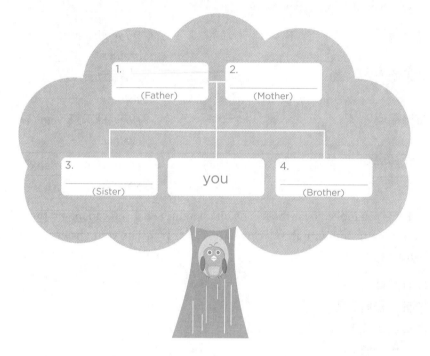

1. _____ (Father)

2. _____ (Mother)

3. _____ (Sister)

you

4. _____ (Brother)

ANSWER KEY
1. fùqīn; 2. mǔqīn; 3. jiějie; 4. gēge

Take It Further 2

Let's practice family characters in the question Nǐ yǒu ... ma? 你有 ... 吗? (*Do you have ...?*) You already know nǐ 你 (*you*) and the question particle ma 吗. The only new character there is the verb yǒu 有 (*have*). Does it remind you of a shelf, where you keep the things you have?

你有哥哥吗?	Nǐ yǒu gēge ma?	*Do you have an older brother?*
你有姐姐吗?	Nǐ yǒu jiějie ma?	*Do you have an older sister?*
你有弟弟吗?	Nǐ yǒu dìdi ma?	*Do you have a younger brother?*
你有妹妹吗?	Nǐ yǒu mèimei ma?	*Do you have a younger sister?*

Great. Have you looked over those new characters? See if you can match the characters on the left with the pīnyīn on the right. Translate your answers into English as well.

1. 你有妹妹吗?	a. Nǐ yǒu dìdi ma?
2. 你有哥哥吗?	b. Nǐ yǒu mèimei ma?
3. 你有弟弟吗?	c. Nǐ yǒu gēge ma?
4. 你有姐姐吗?	d. Nǐ yǒu jiějie ma?

ANSWER KEY

1. b. (*Do you have a younger sister?*) 2. c. (*Do you have an older brother?*) 3. a. (*Do you have a younger brother?*) 4. d. (*Do you have an older sister?*)

Grammar Builder 2

2E Grammar Builder 2 (CD 1, Track 14)

You've already learned how to say *to be* in Chinese—*to have* is just as easy.

to have	yǒu	有
I have	wǒ yǒu	我有
you have	nǐ yǒu	你有
he has	tā yǒu	他有
she has	tā yǒu	她有
we have	wǒmen yǒu	我们有
you (plural) have	nǐmen yǒu	你们有
they have	tāmen yǒu	他们有

The sentence structure for *to have* is just the same as *to be*. Simply place the verb yǒu 有 after the noun or pronoun, and follow it with whatever is being possessed.

I have an older brother.	Wǒ yǒu gēge.	我有哥哥。
You have a younger brother.	Nǐ yǒu dìdi.	你有弟弟。
He has an older sister.	Tā yǒu jiějie.	他有姐姐。
She has a younger sister.	Tā yǒu mèimei.	她有妹妹。

To turn these sentences into questions, simply place ma 吗 at the end of the sentence.

you have	nǐ yǒu	你有
Do you have … ?	Nǐ yǒu … ma?	你有 … 吗?
You have a son.	Nǐ yǒu érzi.	你有儿子。
Do you have a son?	Nǐ yǒu érzi ma?	你有儿子吗?
She has a daughter.	Tā yǒu nǚ'ér.	她有女儿。
Does she have a daughter?	Tā yǒu nǚ'ér ma?	她有女儿吗?

✎ Work Out 1

Let's practice some listening comprehension. Listen to the audio, and fill in the missing words in pīnyīn.

▷ 2F Work Out 1 (CD 1, Track 15)

1. *She is a woman.*

   Tā shì _____.

   她是女人。

2. *He is a man.*

   Tā shì _____.

   他是男人。

3. *The teacher is a woman.*

   _____ nǚrén.

   老师是女人。

4. *The student is a man.*

   _____ shì nánrén.

   学生是男人。

5. *I have an older brother.*

   Wǒ _____ gēge.

   我有哥哥。

6. *You have a younger brother.*

   Nǐ yǒu _____.

   你有弟弟。

7. *He has an older sister.*

Tā yǒu _____.

他有姐姐。

8. *She has a younger sister.*

_____ yǒu _____.

她有妹妹。

9. *Is the teacher a woman?*

Lǎoshī shì nǚrén _____?

老师是女人吗？

10. *Does she have a daughter?*

Tā yǒu _____ ma?

她有女儿吗?

11. *Is the student a man?*

Xuésheng _____ ma?

学生是男人吗？

12. *Does he have a younger brother?*

_____ yǒu _____ ma?

他有弟弟吗?

ANSWER KEY

1. nǚrén; 2. nánrén; 3. Lǎoshī shì; 4. Xuésheng; 5. yǒu; 6. dìdi; 7. jiějie; 8. Tā, mèimei; 9. ma; 10. nǚ'ér; 11. shì nánrén; 12. Tā, dìdi

Bring It All Together

▶ 2G Bring It All Together (CD 1, Track 16)

Let's bring it all together in a short exchange.

Shān: Nǐ shì lǎoshī ma?

你是老师吗?

Are you a teacher?

Lǐ: Wǒ shì lǎoshī.

我是老师。

I am a teacher.

Shān: Tā shì xuésheng ma?

她是学生吗?

Is she a student?

Lǐ: Tā shì xuésheng.

她是学生。

She is a student.

Shān: Xuésheng shì nǚrén ma?

学生是女人吗?

Is the student a woman?

Lǐ: Xuésheng shì nánrén.

学生是男人。

The student is a man.

Shān: Tā shì fùqin ma?

他是父亲吗?

Is he the father?

Lǐ: Tā shì gēge.

他是哥哥。

He is the older brother.

Shān: Nǐ shì mǔqīn ma?

你是母亲吗?

Are you the mother?

Lǐ: Wǒ shì jiějie.
我是姐姐。
I am the older sister.

Very nice. Hěn hǎo. 很好。 Now, we'll work on *to have* 有 (yǒu).

Shān: Nǐ yǒu érzi ma?
你有儿子吗?
Do you have a son?

Lǐ: Wǒ yǒu nǚ'ér.
我有女儿。
I have a daughter.

Shān: Xuésheng yǒu gēge ma?
学生有哥哥吗?
Does the student have an older brother?

Lǐ: Xuésheng yǒu dìdi.
学生有弟弟。
The student has a younger brother.

Shān: Fùqin yǒu jiějie ma?
父亲有姐姐吗?
Does the father have an older sister?

Lǐ: Fùqin yǒu mèimei.
父亲有妹妹。
The father has a younger sister.

(II)

✎ Work Out 2

A. Translate each sentence into English.

1. Wǒ yǒu mǔqīn. _____

_____

2. Tā yǒu fùqin. _____

_____

3. Tā yǒu jiějie. _____

_____

4. Wǒmen yǒu nǚ'er. _____

_____

B. Let's do the reverse. Now translate each sentence into pīnyīn.

1. *Is she the mother?* _____

_____

2. *Is he the father?* _____

_____

3. *Are you a student?* _____

_____

4. *Are you a teacher?* _____

_____

ANSWER KEY

A. 1. *I have a mother.* 2. *She/he has a father.* 3. *He/she has an older sister.* 4. *We have a daughter.*

B. 1. Tā shì mǔqin ma? 2. Tā shì fùqin ma? 3. Nǐ shì xuésheng ma? 4. Nǐ shì lǎoshī ma?

▶ 2H Work Out 2 (CD 1, Track 17)

Now listen to your audio for some additional audio-only practice.

⏸

✎ Drive It Home

Let's do another Drive It Home exercise. Remember, even though these exercises may seem to be easy and repetitive, they're very important because they'll help you make Chinese grammar more automatic. Ready?

First, form sentences using Wǒ yǒu … 我有 … (*I have …*) with each of the family terms below. Write out each sentence in pīnyīn, and say it aloud as you read it.

Wǒ yǒu _____.

我有 _____ 。

… mǔqīn 母亲 (*a mother*), … fùqin 父亲 (*a father*), … nǚ'ér 女儿 (*a daughter*), … érzi 儿子 (*a son*).

Now ask if the student has different siblings, using the model below:

Xuésheng yǒu _____ ma?

学生有 _____ 吗?

mèimei 妹妹 (*younger sister*)

jiějie 姐姐 (*older sister*)

dìdi 弟弟 (*younger brother*)

gēge 哥哥 (*older brother*)

Parting words

▶ 21 Parting Words (CD 1, Track 18)

Well done! Before you go, here are a few more words you may use every day when talking about people you know and family members.

Mr./husband	xiānsheng	先生
Mrs./wife	tàitai	太太
Miss/young lady	xiǎojiě	小姐
boy	nánhái	男孩
girl	nǚhái	女孩

⏸

And now, you've reached the end of your second lesson of *Essential Chinese*! Here's what you focused on in this lesson:

☐ Basic vocabulary for talking about people. (Still unsure? Go back to 26.)

☐ The verb *to be* and the pronouns *I, you, he, she,* and so on.
(Still unsure? Go back to 28.)

☐ Key vocabulary related to the family. (Still unsure? Go back to 30.)

☐ The verb *to have*. (Still unsure? Go back to 33.)

☐ A few short conversations about people and the family.
(Still unsure? Go back to 36.)

Don't forget to practice and reinforce what you've learned by visiting **www.livinglanguage.com/languagelab** for flashcards, games, and quizzes for Lesson Two!

Word Recall

Match the English word in column A with its appropriate translation in column B.

1. *very*	a. dìdi 弟弟
2. *female*	b. hǎo 好
3. *good, fine*	c. rén 人
4. *to be*	d. jiějie 姐姐
5. *thanks*	e. nǚ 女
6. *teacher*	f. hěn 很
7. *they, them*	g. mǔqīn 母亲
8. *younger brother*	h. duìbùqǐ 对不起
9. *I am sorry*	i. shì 是
10. *person, people*	j. tāmen 他们
11. *older sister*	k. lǎoshī 老师
12. *mother*	l. xièxie 谢谢

ANSWER KEY
1. f; 2. e; 3. b; 4. i; 5. l; 6. k; 7. j; 8. a; 9. h; 10. c; 11. d; 12. g

Character Recall

Now let's review the characters you focused on in these first two lessons. First, match the characters for brothers and sisters on the left to the pīnyīn and translation on the right.

1. 弟弟	a. gēge (*older brother*)
2. 姐姐	b. dìdi (*younger brother*)
3. 妹妹	c. jiějie (*older sister*)
4. 哥哥	d. mèimei (*younger sister*)

ANSWER KEY
1. b; 2. c. 3; d; 4. a.

Great. Now, do the same with the pronouns.

1. 我们	a. wǒ (*I*)
2. 他	b. tā (*she, her*)
3. 你	c. tāmen (*they, them*)
4. 我	d. wǒmen (*we, us*)
5. 他们	e. nǐmen (*you, plural*)
6. 她	f. tā (*he, him*)
7. 你们	g. nǐ (*you*)

ANSWER KEY
1. d; 2. f; 3. g; 4. a; 5. c; 6. b; 7. e

And finally, here are some other types of characters you've focused on.

1. 好	a. xièxie (*thanks*)
2. 谢谢	b. hěn (*very*)
3. 吗	c. ma (*question particle*)
4. 有	d. hǎo (*good, fine*)
5. 很	e. yǒu (*have*)

ANSWER KEY
1. d; 2. a; 3. c; 4. e; 5. b

Lesson 3: Numbers

Dì-sān kè: Shùzì

第三课：数字

Welcome to your third lesson of *Essential Chinese*. You'll continue to build your vocabulary and knowledge of Chinese by focusing on:

☐ Numbers in the ones, teens, and tens.

☐ How to use them along with measure words.

☐ More numbers, all the way up to one million.

☐ How to express more than one of something.

☐ How to put it all together in a longer monologue.

Vocabulary Builder 1

▶ 3B Vocabulary Builder 1 (CD 1, Track 20)

zero	líng	零
one	yī	一
two	èr	二
three	sān	三
four	sì	四
five	wǔ	五
six	liù	六
seven	qī	七
eight	bā	八
nine	jiǔ	九
ten	shí	十

Now let's move on to the teens. From 11 to 19, you will say *ten* first, then follow it by *one* through *nine*. *Eleven* will be *ten one*, *twelve* will be *ten two*, and so on.

eleven	shíyī	十一
twelve	shí'èr	十二
thirteen	shísān	十三
nineteen	shíjiǔ	十九

The tens are the reverse of the teens. You say the *two* through *nine* first, and add *ten* to it. *Twenty* will be *two ten*, *thirty* will be *three ten*, and so on.

20	èrshí	二十
30	sānshí	三十
40	sìshí	四十
90	jiǔshí	九十

⏸

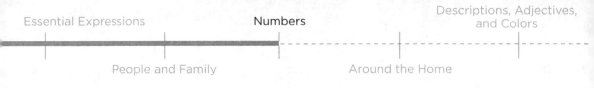
✎ Vocabulary Practice 1

Let's do some simple math to practice the numbers. Write out the pīnyīn answer to each of the following.

1. yī 一 + sān 三 = _____ 四。

2. wǔ 五 + wǔ 五 = _____ 十。

3. liù 六 – sì 四 = _____ 二。

4. wǔ 五 + èr 二 = _____ 七。

5. jiǔ 九 – bā 八 = _____ 一。

6. èr 二 × sān 三 = _____ 六。

ANSWER KEY
1. sì; 2. shí; 3. èr; 4. qī; 5. yī; 6. liù

Take It Further 1

Okay, let's take a closer look at all of the characters for yī 一 through shí 十. Remembering the first three shouldn't give you any trouble at all; they're simply one, two, and three horizontal strokes:

一	yī	*one*
二	èr	*two*
三	sān	*three*

The character for *four* is a four-sided box, and you can almost see the number 4 if you look at the right side and the stroke that comes into it. *Five* is a bit trickier, but again, if you look closely enough, you can see something like a 5 on the right-hand side. *Six* looks like a person walking, although you'll have to come up with your own mnemonic as to why that has anything to do with six!

四	sì	*four*
五	wǔ	*five*
六	liù	*six*

Seven looks a little bit like a boat with a mast, maybe one to sail the seven seas. *Eight* looks a bit like a capital *A*, as in *Ate*. *Nine* is tricky, although it's got two vertical strokes, similar to eight, and then adds one horizontal stroke, and 8 + 1 = 9. Finally, when you write the number 10, it's the first number where you add a zero, so the fact that it looks like a big plus sign might help.

七	qī	*seven*
八	bā	*eight*
九	jiǔ	*nine*
十	shí	*ten*

Of course, these mnemonics are just suggestions. If they work for you, that's great. If not, it will be helpful for you to come up with your own. Go back and read over the numbers yī 一 through shí 十 one more time, and then see what you remember. Write out the pīnyīn and translation for the following.

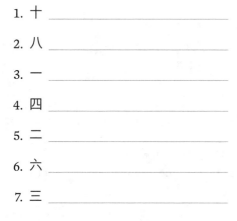

1. 十 _____

2. 八 _____

3. 一 _____

4. 四 _____

5. 二 _____

6. 六 _____

7. 三 _____

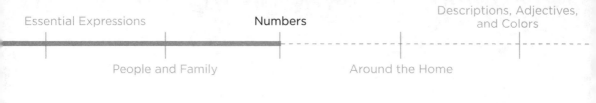

8. 七 _____

9. 五 _____

10. 九 _____

ANSWER KEY
1. shí (*ten*); 2. bā (*eight*); 3. yī (*one*); 4. sì (*four*); 5. èr (*two*); 6. liù (*six*); 7. sān (*three*); 8. qī (*seven*);
9. wǔ (*five*); 10. jiǔ (*nine*)

Now is a good time to go to your *Guide to Chinese Characters* and read Lesson Three: Turning Strokes. If you go back to Lesson One: Basic Strokes, you can practice the characters for *one, two, three,* and *ten* as well.

Grammar Builder 1

▶ 3C Grammar Builder 1 (CD 1, Track 21)

Let's pause for a moment to learn about how to deal with quantity. Chinese uses measure words, words that come between the numbers and the items, when talking about quantity. Measure words are similar to *pair* in *one pair of shoes* or *glass* in *five glasses of wine,* but every noun in Chinese requires a measure word when talking about its quantity. Let's learn the most general one first.

People, cities, groups, and nations use the measure word gè 个:

one woman	yī gè nǚrén	一个女人
ten students	shí gè xuésheng	十个学生
twelve teachers	shí'èr gè lǎoshī	十二个老师
twenty men	èrshí gè nánrén	二十个男人

One note regarding the number *two;* when you use two as an amount, the pronunciation changes to liǎng 两. This applies to the number *two,* but not to numbers that include two, such as 32, 42, 52, etc.

| two teachers | liǎng gè lǎoshī | 两个老师 |
| two women | liǎng gè nǚrén | 两个女人 |

Vocabulary Builder 2

3D Vocabulary Builder 2 (CD 1, Track 22)

Very good. Hěn hǎo. 很好。 Now let's go back to more numbers. From 21 to 99, you just add *one* to *nine* after the tens.

21	èrshíyī	二十一
22	èrshí'èr	二十二
23	èrshísān	二十三
34	sānshísì	三十四
45	sìshíwǔ	四十五
56	wǔshíliù	五十六
67	liùshíqī	六十七
78	qīshíbā	七十八
89	bāshíjiǔ	八十九
99	jiǔshíjiǔ	九十九

After *ninety-nine*, we have *hundred* (bǎi 百), *thousand* (qiān 千), *ten thousand* (wàn 万), and so on.

one hundred	yībǎi	一百
one thousand	yīqiān	一千
ten thousand	yīwàn	一万
one million	yībǎi wàn	一百万

Note that wàn 万 is treated as its own unit, like *hundred*, *thousand*, or *million*. So 10,000 is *ten thousand* in English, but *one* wàn in Chinese.

Ⓘ

✎ Vocabulary Practice 2

Let's do some simple math with bigger numbers. Write out the pīnyīn answer to each of the following:

1. sānshí 三十 + liùshí 六十 = _____ 九十.

2. qīshí 七十 – wǔ 五 = _____ 六十五.

3. èrshísān 二十三 + sānshísān 三十三 = _____ 五十六.

4. shí 十 + jiǔshí 十 = _____ 一百.

5. bāshí'èr 八十二 – qīshísān 七十三 = _____ 九.

6. sìshísì 四十四 + shísì 十四 = _____ 五十八.

ANSWER KEY
1. jiǔshí; 2. liùshíwǔ; 3. wǔshíliù; 4. yībǎi; 5. jiǔ; 6. wǔshíbā

Take It Further 2

Since we covered the most important number characters in Take It Further 1, let's go back to a few more basic characters for people. Notice that rén 人 (*person*) looks a bit like a stick figure standing, at least without the arms. That same character appears in nǚrén 女人 (*woman*) and nánrén 男人 (*man*). The characters 女 and 男 mean *female* and *male*, respectively, and you can also see them in nǚhái 女孩 (*girl*) and nánhái 男孩 (*boy*). Look over these characters, and try to come up with a few mnemonics of your own.

人	rén	*person, people*
女人	nǚrén	*woman*
男人	nánrén	*man*
男孩	nánhái	*boy*

| 女孩 | nǚhái | *girl* |

Can you recognize those characters? Let's do a quick check. Match the characters in the left column with the pīnyīn on the right, and then translate them into English.

1. 男孩	a. rén
2. 人	b. nǚrén
3. 女孩	c. nánrén
4. 女人	d. nánhái
5. 男人	e. nǚhái

ANSWER KEY

1. d (*boy*); 2. a (*person, people*); 3. e (*girl*); 4. b (*woman*); 5. c (*man*)

Now let's make this a little more challenging and recycle some of the characters for pronouns that you learned earlier. Remember that shì 是 means *am, is,* or *are.* Can you read the following simple sentences?

1. 他是男孩。 _____

2. 我是女人。 _____

3. 你是男人。 _____

4. 她是女孩。 _____

ANSWER KEY

1. Tā shì nánhái. (*He is a boy.*) 2. Wǒ shì nǚrén. (*I am a woman.*) 3. Nǐ shì nánrén. (*You are a man.*)
4. Tā shì nǚhái. (*She is a girl.*)

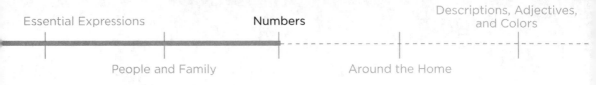
Grammar Builder 2

▶ 3E Grammar Builder 2 (CD 1, Track 23)

Here's some more good news: In Chinese, there is no plural form for either nouns or their measure words. That means when the quantity changes, the noun and its measure word stay the same.

one older brother	yī gè gēge	一个哥哥
two older brothers	liǎng gè gēge	两个哥哥
three younger brothers	sān gè dìdi	三个弟弟
four younger brothers	sì gè dìdi	四个弟弟
five teachers	wǔ gè lǎoshī	五个老师
six teachers	liù gè lǎoshī	六个老师
seven teachers	qī gè lǎoshī	七个老师
eight students	bā gè xuésheng	八个学生
nine students	jiǔ gè xuésheng	九个学生

⏸

✎ Work Out 1

Let's do some listening comprehension practice. Listen to the audio and fill in the missing pīnyīn.

▶ 3F Work Out 1 (CD 1, Track 24)

1. *I have one older brother.*

   Wǒ yǒu _____ gēge.

   我有一个哥哥。

At a Restaurant

At Work

Review Dialogues

Around Town

Everyday Life

Socializing

2. *He has two older brothers.*

Tā yǒu _____ gè gēge.

他有两个哥哥 。

3. *You have three younger brothers.*

Nǐ _____ sān _____ dìdi.

你有三个弟弟。

4. *She has four younger brothers.*

Tā yǒu _____ dìdi.

她有四个弟弟。

5. *I have five teachers.*

_____ yǒu wǔ gè _____.

我有五个老师.

6. *He has six teachers.*

Tā yǒu _____ lǎoshī.

他有六个老师。

7. *You have seven teachers.*

Nǐ yǒu _____ gè lǎoshī.

你有七个老师。

8. *She has eight students.*

Tā yǒu _____ gè _____.

她有八个学生。

9. *You have nine students.*

Nǐ yǒu _____ lǎoshī.

你有九个学生。

ANSWER KEY

1. yī gè; 2. liǎng; 3. yǒu, gè; 4. sì gè; 5. Wǒ, lǎoshī; 6. liù, gè; 7. qī; 8. bā, xuésheng; 9. jiǔ gè

Bring It All Together

▶ 3G Bring It All Together (CD 1, Track 25)

Now we'll bring it all together by listening to a short monologue. You'll hear it in English and Chinese first. Repeat after the Chinese.

Wǒ yǒu sì gè lǎoshī.

我有四个老师。

I have four teachers.

Liǎng gè lǎoshī shì nánrén.

两个老师是男人。

Two teachers are men.

Liǎng gè lǎoshī shì nǚrén.

两个老师是女人。

Two teachers are women.

Fùqin yǒu sān gè gēge.

父亲有三个哥哥。

Father has three older brothers.

Yī gè gēge shì lǎoshī.

一个哥哥是老师。

One older brother is a teacher.

Tā yǒu bāshí gè xuésheng.

他有八十个学生。

He has 80 students.

Èrshíwǔ gè xuésheng shì nǚrén.

二十五个学生是女人。

Twenty-five students are women.

✎ Work Out 2

Now let's practice. Match the English phrase on the left with the Chinese on the right.

1. *two younger brothers*	a. yī gè xuésheng 一个学生
2. *four teachers*	b. liǎng gè dìdi 两个弟弟
3. *one student*	c. sān gè gēge 三个哥哥
4. *seven older sisters*	d. sì gè lǎoshī 四个老师
5. *three older brothers*	e. qī gè jiějie 七个姐姐

ANSWER KEY

1. b; 2. d; 3. a; 4. e; 5. c

▶ 3H Work Out 2 (CD 1, Track 26)

Now listen to your audio for some audio-only practice and review with numbers and measure words for people.

✏ Drive It Home

Now it's time to drive home the pattern of using the measure word gè 个. For each noun given, form phrases including the numbers yī 一 through wǔ 五. For example, with gēge 哥哥, you'd write out and say:

yī gè gēge, liǎng gè gēge, sān gè gēge, sì gè gēge, wǔ gè gēge

Now do the same thing with:

rén 人 _____

_____

nǚrén 女人 _____

_____

nánrén 男人 _____

_____

dìdi 弟弟 _____

_____

lǎoshī 老师 _____

_____

xuésheng 学生 _____

_____

Parting Words

Take a look at the characters for the numbers one through ten one more time.

一, 二, 三, 四, 五, 六, 七, 八, 九, 十.

By now, you know how to pronounce them, too: yī, èr, sān, sì, wǔ, liù, qī, bā, jiǔ, shí. And that brings us to the end of Lesson 3 of *Essential Chinese*. You should know:

☐ Numbers in the ones, teens, and tens.
  (Still unsure? Go back to 45.)

☐ How to use them along with measure words.
  (Still unsure? Go back to 48.)

☐ More numbers, all the way up to one million.
  (Still unsure? Go back to 49.)

☐ How to express more than one of something.
  (Still unsure? Go back to 52.)

☐ How to put it all together in a longer monologue.
  (Still unsure? Go back to 54.)

Don't forget to practice and reinforce what you've learned by visiting **www.livinglanguage.com/languagelab** for flashcards, games, and quizzes for Lesson Three!

Word Recall

Let's review some of the key vocabulary you've learned so far. Match the English on the left to the pīnyīn and characters on the right. How many of the characters do you recognize?

1. *I*	a. méi shì 没事
2. *student*	b. fùqin 父亲
3. *six*	c. wǒ 我
4. *(measure word for people, cities, groups, and nations)*	d. xuésheng 学生
5. *one hundred*	e. líng 零
6. *three*	f. liù 六
7. *father*	g. yībǎi 一百
8. *It's nothing.*	h. gè 个
9. *daughter*	i. zài jiàn 再见
10. *nine*	j. liǎng 两
11. *goodbye*	k. sān 三
12. *zero*	l. jiǔ 九
13. *two (used to describe amount)*	m. shí 十
14. *woman*	n. nǚrén 女人
15. *ten*	o. nǚ'ér 女儿

ANSWER KEY
1. c; 2. d; 3. f; 4. h; 5. g; 6. k; 7. b; 8. a; 9. o; 10. l; 11. i; 12. e; 13. j; 14. n; 15. m

Character Recall

And now, let's make sure the major characters we've focused on remain fresh in your mind. We'll review the characters for people that you've learned so far. Match the character on the left with the pīnyīn and translation on the right.

1. 男孩	a. nánrén (*man*)
2. 妹妹	b. jiějie (*older sister*)
3. 男人	c. nǚhái (*girl*)
4. 弟弟	d. dìdi (*younger brother*)
5. 人	e. nǚrén (*woman*)
6. 姐姐	f. mèimei (*younger sister*)
7. 哥哥	g. nánhái (*boy*)
8. 女孩	h. rén (*person, people*)
9. 女人	i. gēge (*older brother*)

ANSWER KEY
1. g; 2. f; 3. a; 4. d; 5. h; 6. b; 7. i; 8. c; 9. e

Lesson 4: Around the Home

Dì-sì kè: Jiājù

第四课: 家具

Are you ready for your fourth lesson of *Essential Chinese*? In this lesson, you'll learn:

☐ The names of common items found around the home.

☐ How to ask questions with *who*.

☐ More common measure words.

☐ How to use them to talk about everyday objects.

☐ How to bring it all together in a short dialogue.

At a Restaurant

At Work

Review Dialogues

Around Town

Everyday Life

Socializing

Vocabulary Builder 1

4B Vocabulary Builder 1 (CD 1, Track 28)

table	zhuōzi	桌子
chair	yǐzi	椅子
television	diànshì	电视
telephone	diànhuà	电话
computer	diànnǎo	电脑
refrigerator	bīngxiāng	冰箱
book	shū	书
car	qìchē	汽车
bicycle	zìxíngchē	自行车

Vocabulary Practice 1

Let's practice that new vocabulary. Match the English on the left with the Chinese on the right.

1. book	a. qìchē 汽车
2. car	b. zhuōzi 桌子
3. computer	c. shū 书
4. table	d. zìxíngchē 自行车
5. bicycle	e. bīngxiāng 冰箱
6. refrigerator	f. diànnǎo 电脑

ANSWER KEY
1. c; 2. a; 3. f; 4. b; 5. d; 6. e

Take It Further 1

Now let's focus on a few characters for common items around the home. The character 电 diàn has to do with electricity. If you stretch your imagination a little bit, it might remind you of a kite with a tail on it, and that might remind you of the story of Ben Franklin and the lightning. But that's just a suggestion! Notice that 电 diàn appears in three very common household objects, all of which use electricity.

电视	diànshì	*television*
电话	diànhuà	*telephone*
电脑	diànnǎo	*computer*

Take a look at each of those three, and pay attention to what follows 电 diàn in each case. Can you see anything that will help you remember them? Something that looks like a person 人 silhouetted in front of a box, as if watching television? The top of a telephone pole? A complex boxy-looking contraption, like a CPU? With those mnemonics in mind, what do these characters mean?

1. 电话 _____

2. 电脑 _____

3. 电视 _____

ANSWER KEY

1. diànhuà (*telephone*); 2. diànnǎo (*computer*); 3. diànshì (*television*)

Now go to your *Guide to Chinese Characters* and read Lesson Four: More Turning Strokes.

Grammar Builder 1

▶ 4C Grammar Builder 1 (CD 1, Track 29)

The question word shéi 谁 (who, whom) can be used as the subject, who, or the object of a verb, whom, and can be used as singular or plural. Let's look at it as the subject for now.

When using the question word shéi 谁, you don't need to end the sentence with ma 吗. And in the answer, the pronoun will replace shéi 谁.

Don't forget your pronouns: wǒ 我, nǐ 你, tā 他/她, wǒmen 我们, nǐmen 你们, tāmen 他们.

Who has tables?	Shéi yǒu zhuōzi?	谁有桌子？
She has a table.	Tā yǒu yī zhāng zhuōzi.	她有一张桌子。

Who has a telephone?	Shéi yǒu diànhuà?	谁有电话？
You (plural) have a telephone.	Nǐmen yǒu diànhuà.	你们有电话。

Who has a computer?	Shéi yǒu diànnǎo?	谁有电脑？
They have a computer.	Tāmen yǒu diànnǎo.	他们有电脑。

Who has a book?	Shéi yǒu běn shū?	谁有本书？
He has a book.	Tā yǒu běn shū.	他有本书。

Who has a car?	Shéi yǒu qìchē?	谁有汽车？
We have a car.	Wǒmen yǒu qìchē.	我们有汽车。

⏸

Vocabulary Builder 2

▶ 4D Vocabulary Builder 2 (CD 1, Track 30)

In the last lesson, you learned about measure words. Measure words come in groups, based on different qualities of the object being counted. Let's learn some more of these measure words, related to words you've learned so far in this lesson.

books, photo albums, magazines	běn	本
cars, taxis, bicycles	liàng	辆
machines	tái	台
tables, desks, chairs	zhāng	张

✎ Vocabulary Practice 2

Let's practice the measure words you've seen so far. For each item in the left column, first give the translation, and then find the correct measure word that you'd use with it from the right column.

1. qìchē 汽车	a. tái 台
2. shū 书	b. zhāng 张
3. xuésheng 学生	c. liàng 辆
4. zhuōzi 桌子	d. gè 个
5. diànnǎo 电脑	e. běn 本

ANSWER KEY

1. c (*cars*); 2. e (*books*); 3. d (*students*); 4. b (*tables*); 5. a (*computers*)

Take It Further 2

Okay, let's take another look at some common objects from around the home. Notice that zhuōzi (*table*) 桌子 and yǐzi (*chair*) 椅子 both include 子. You might be able to see something in 桌子 that reminds you of a table, seen from the side. Study these characters, and, as always, look for any images or suggestions that will help remind you of their meanings.

桌子	zhuōzi	*table*
椅子	yǐzi	*chair*
书	shū	*book*
汽车	qìchē	*car*

Okay, let's review these, as well as the three characters we focused on earlier in this lesson. Match the character on the left with the pīnyīn and translation on the right.

1. 汽车	a. shū (*book*)
2. 电话	b. diànshì (*television*)
3. 书	c. yǐzi (*chair*)
4. 电视	d. qìchē (*car*)
5. 桌子	e. diànnǎo (*computer*)
6. 椅子	f. zhuōzi (*table*)
7. 电脑	g. diànhuà (*telephone*)

ANSWER KEY
1. d; 2. g; 3. a; 4. b; 5. f; 6. c; 7. e

Grammar Builder 2

▶ 4E Grammar Builder 2 (CD 1, Track 31)

Now let's take a closer look at these measure words in use. The measure word used for books, photo albums, or magazines is běn 本.

| *I have two books.* | Wǒ yǒu liǎng běn shū. | 我有两本书. |

Notice that in this phrase you are using the word for two, liǎng 两, the measure word běn 本, followed by the word for book, shū 书.

The measure word for cars, taxis, and bicycles is liàng 辆.

| *We have nine cars.* | Wǒmen yǒu jiǔ liàng chē. | 我们有九辆车。 |
| *She has ten bicycles.* | Tā yǒu shí liàng zìxíngchē. | 她有十辆自行车。 |

The measure word for machines, such as sewing machines, televisions, or air conditioners, is tái 台.

You (plural) have four telephones.	Nǐmen yǒu sì tái diànhuà.	你们有四台电话。
You (singular) have five televisions.	Nǐ yǒu wǔ tái diànshì.	你有五台电视。
I have six computers.	Wǒ yǒu liù tái diànnǎo.	我有六台电脑。
They have seven refrigerators.	Tāmen yǒu qī tái bīngxiāng.	他们有七台冰箱。

The measure word for tables, desks, and chairs is zhāng 张.

| *She has one table.* | Tā yǒu yī zhāng zhuōzi. | 她有一张桌子。 |
| *We have two chairs.* | Wǒmen yǒu liǎng zhāng yǐzi. | 我们有两张椅子。 |

Ⅱ

✎ Work Out 1

Let's do a listening comprehension exercise, focusing on measure words and vocabulary for common objects. Before we begin, though, note that the word for *and* (hé 和) is commonly omitted in Chinese, especially when you're listing more than two items. So, in the English translations, you'll see *and* in parentheses, but it's not actually used in the Chinese.

▶ 4F Work Out 1 (CD 1, Track 32)

1. *You have three cars.*

   Nǐ yǒu _____ qìchē.

   你有三辆汽车。

2. *I have two cars.*

   Wǒ yǒu liǎng _____.

   我有两辆汽车。

3. *We have five cars.*

   Wǒmen yǒu _____ qìchē.

   我们有五辆汽车。

4. *Mother has one computer (and) five books.*

   Mǔqīn yǒu yī _____, wǔ _____ shū.

   母亲有一台电脑, 五本书。

5. *The daughter has three computers (and) four books.*

   Nǚ'ér yǒu sān _____ diànnǎo, _____ shū.

   女儿有三台电脑, 四本书。

6. *They have eight computers (and) nine books.*

   Tāmen yǒu _____ diànnǎo, _____ shū.

   他们有八台电脑，九本书。

   ANSWER KEY
   1. sān liàng; 2. liàng qìchē; 3. wǔ liàng; 4. tái diànnǎo, běn; 5. tái, sì běn; 6. bā tái, jiǔ běn

Bring It All Together
4G Bring It All Together (CD 2, Track 1)

Listen to the following dialogue that will bring together everything you've learned so far in this course.

Yáng:	Shéi yǒu diànshì?
	谁有电视？
	Who has a television?
Yù:	Mèimei yǒu yī tái diànshì.
	妹妹有一台电视。
	Younger sister has one television.
Yáng:	Tā yǒu zhuōzi, yǐzi ma?
	她有桌子椅子吗？
	Does she have tables and chairs?
Yù:	Tā yǒu sān zhāng zhuōzi, liù zhāng yǐzi.
	她有三张桌子，六张椅子。
	She has three tables, six chairs.
Yáng:	Shéi yǒu liǎng tái bīngxiāng?
	谁有两台冰箱？
	Who has two refrigerators?
Yù:	Lǎoshī yǒu.
	老师有。
	The teacher does. (lit., The teacher has.)

At a Restaurant

At Work

Review Dialogues

Around Town

Everyday Life

Socializing

Yáng:	Lǎoshī shì shéi?
	老师是谁?
	Who is the teacher?
Yù:	Lǎoshī shì wǒ.
	老师是我。
	I'm the teacher. (lit., The teacher is me.)

✎ Work Out 2

Choose the best word to complete each sentence.

1. Wǒ yǒu yī běn _____. (*I have one book.*)

   a. diànshì

   b. shū

   c. yǐzi

   d. bīngxiāng

2. Lǎoshī yǒu liǎng tái _____. (*The teacher has two computers.*)

   a. qìchē

   b. zhuōzi

   c. diànnǎo

   d. zìxíngchē

3. Dìdi yǒu bā liàng _____. (*Younger brother has eight bicycles.*)

   a. diànhuà

   b. diànnǎo

   c. zìxíngchē

   d. shū

4. Tāmen yǒu shíqī _____ zhuōzi. (*They have seventeen tables.*)

 a. tái

 b. běn

 c. liàng

 d. zhāng

5. Fùqin yǒu yī _____ lǎoshī. (*Father has one teacher.*)

 a. gè

 b. zhāng

 c. běn

 d. tái

6. Nímen yǒu yī _____ qìchē ma? (*Do you have a car?*)

 a. zhāng

 b. liàng

 c. gè

 d. běn

7. Wǒmen shì sān _____ mǔqīn. (*We are three mothers.*)

 a. gè

 b. tái

 c. liàng

 d. zhāng

8. Mèimei yǒu wǔ zhāng _____. (*Younger sister has five chairs.*)

 a. diànshì

 b. bīngxiāng

 c. yǐzi

 d. diànnǎo

9. Nánhái yǒu jiǔ tái _____. (*The boy has nine telephones.*)

   a. zìxíngchē

   b. bīngxiāng

   c. diànhuà

   d. shū

10. Shéi yǒu qī tái _____? (*Who has seven refrigerators?*)

   a. qìchē

   b. zhuōzi

   c. diànshì

   d. bīngxiāng

ANSWER KEY
1. b; 2. c; 3. c; 4. d; 5. a; 6. b; 7. a; 8. c; 9. c; 10. d

▶ 4H Work Out 2 (CD 2, Track 2)

Now listen to your recordings for some audio-only practice and review.

⏸

✎ Drive It Home

Now it's time to drive home the pattern of using the measure words běn 本, liàng 辆, tái 台, and zhāng 张. For each noun given, form phrases including the numbers yī 一 through wǔ 五. For example, with diànshì 电视, you'd write out and say:

yī tái diànshì, liǎng tái diànshì, sān tái diànshì, sì tái diànshì, wǔ tái diànshì

Now do the same thing with:

liàng 辆: zìxíngchē 自行车, qìchē 汽车

zhāng 张: zhuōzi 桌子, yǐzi 椅子

Lesson 4: Around the Home   71

běn 本: shū 书

tái 台: diànnǎo 电脑, diànhuà 电话, bīngxiāng 冰箱

Parting Words

Congratulations. Gōngxǐ nǐ. 恭喜你。 You've finished Lesson 4, which means that you should know:

- ☐ The names of common items found around the home.
  (Still unsure? Go back to 61.)

- ☐ How to ask questions with *who*.
  (Still unsure? Go back to 63.)

- ☐ More common measure words.
  (Still unsure? Go back to 64.)

- ☐ How to use them to talk about everyday objects.
  (Still unsure? Go back to 66.)

- ☐ How to bring it all together in a short dialogue.
  (Still unsure? Go back to 68.)

Don't forget to practice and reinforce what you've learned by visiting **www.livinglanguage.com/languagelab** for flashcards, games, and quizzes for Lesson Four!

Word Recall

Let's practice some of the vocabulary you've learned over the past few lessons. Match the English on the left with the Chinese on the right.

1. *one thousand*	a. bīngxiāng 冰箱
2. *car*	b. yǐzi 椅子
3. *table*	c. běn 本
4. *ten thousand*	d. qìchē 汽车
5. *chair*	e. diànhuà 电话
6. *book*	f. diànshì 电视
7. *measure word for tables, desks, chairs*	g. tái 台
8. *television*	h. yīqiān 一千
9. *telephone*	i. shū 书
10. *bicycle*	j. liàng 辆
11. *computer*	k. zìxíngchē 自行车
12. *measure word for books, photo albums, magazines*	l. yīwàn 一万
13. *measure word for cars, taxis, bicycles*	m. zhāng 张
14. *refrigerator*	n. zhuōzi 桌子
15. *measure word for machines*	o. diànnǎo 电脑

ANSWER KEY
1. h; 2. d; 3. n; 4. l; 5. b; 6. i; 7. m; 8. f; 9. e; 10. k; 11. o; 12. c; 13. j; 14. a; 15. g

Character Recall

Let's review the key characters you've focused on in the Take It Further sections so far. First, match these characters for people to their pīnyīn and translations.

1. 女人	a. nánhái (*boy*)
2. 男孩	b. nǚhái (*girl*)
3. 女孩	c. nǚrén (*woman*)
4. 男人	d. nánrén (*man*)

ANSWER KEY
1. c; 2. a; 3. b; 4. d

Now do the same thing with these objects.

1. 电视	a. qìchē (*car*)
2. 汽车	b. diànnǎo (*computer*)
3. 电脑	c. shū (*book*)
4. 椅子	d. diànshì (*television*)
5. 书	e. diànhuà (*telephone*)
6. 电话	f. yǐzi (*chair*)

ANSWER KEY
1. d; 2. a; 3. b; 4. f; 5. c; 6. e

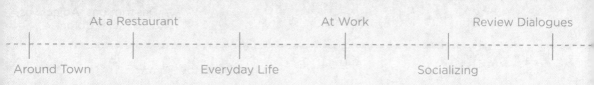
Now let's put all of these together in some sentences. Remember that 有 is the character for yǒu (*have*), as in你有妹妹吗? Nǐ yǒu mèimei ma? (*Do you have a younger sister?*) Let's expand on that pattern, using other characters for people and objects that we just reviewed. Give the pīnyīn and translation for the following questions.

1. 女人有汽车吗? _____

    _____

2. 男孩有书吗? _____

    _____

3. 女孩有电脑吗? _____

    _____

4. 男人有电视吗? _____

    _____

5. 女人有椅子吗? _____

    _____

6. 男孩有电话吗? _____

    _____

ANSWER KEY

1. Nǚrén yǒu qìchē ma? (*Does the woman have a car?*) 2. Nánhái yǒu shū ma? (*Does the boy have a book?*) 3. Nǚhái yǒu diànnǎo ma? (*Does the girl have a computer?*) 4. Nánrén yǒu diànshì ma? (*Does the man have a television?*) 5. Nǚrén yǒu yǐzi ma? (*Does the woman have a chair?*) 6. Nánhái yǒu diànhuà ma? (*Does the boy have a telephone?*)

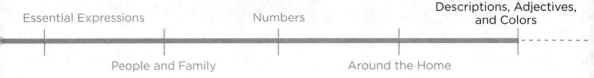

Lesson 5: Descriptions, Adjectives, and Colors

Dì-wǔ kè: Miáoshù, xíngróngcí, yánsè
第五课：描述，形容词，颜色

In this lesson, you'll learn:

☐ More basic vocabulary related to people and things.

☐ How to express possession with the useful particle de 的.

☐ Common adjectives, including colors.

☐ How to use adjectives to describe people and things.

☐ How to put it all together in a few simple sentences.

Vocabulary Builder 1

▶ 5B Vocabulary Builder 1 (CD 2, Track 5)

doctor	yīshēng	医生
nurse	hùshi	护士
police officer	jǐngchá	警察
camera	zhàoxiàngjī	照相机
paper	zhǐ	纸
pen	bǐ	笔
hat	màozi	帽子
coat	wàitào	外套
shoes	xiézi	鞋子

⑪

✎ Vocabulary Practice 1

Let's practice some of that new vocabulary. Fill in the blanks with the missing words, indicated in parentheses, and then translate the full sentence into English.

1. Jǐngchá yǒu _____ . (a pen)

   警察有笔。

2. Hùshi yǒu _____ . (a coat)

   护士有外套。

3. Nǐ yǒu _____ ma? (a hat)

   你有帽子吗?

4. Lǎoshī yǒu _____ . (a camera)

   老师有照相机。

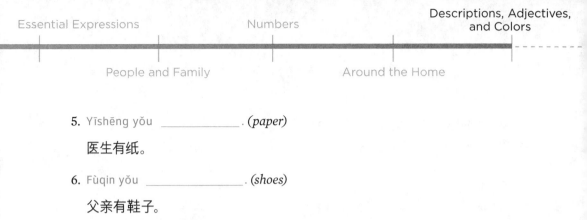

5. Yīshēng yǒu _____ . (*paper*)

医生有纸。

6. Fùqin yǒu _____ . (*shoes*)

父亲有鞋子。

ANSWER KEY
1. bǐ (*The police officer has a pen.*) 2. wàitào (*The nurse has a coat.*) 3. màozi (*Do you have a hat?*)
4. zhàoxiàngjī (*The teacher has a camera.*) 5. zhǐ (*The doctor has paper.*) 6. xiézi (*Father has shoes.*)

Take It Further 1

Okay, now let's stop and take a look at a few new characters. It'll take some imagination to come up with mnemonics for these! But perhaps the cross strokes of 笔 bǐ (*pen*) remind you of the ridges at the tip of an old fountain pen. And notice that 帽子 màozi (*hat*) and 鞋子 xiézi (*shoes*) both include 子, which you saw in the last lesson in the characters 桌子 zhuōzi (*table*) and 椅子 yǐzi (*chair*). Some other possible suggestions: 帽子 includes something that looks like it could be a person standing next to a table with a *hat* box on it. And 鞋子 includes a pair of cross-like strokes, as in a pair of *shoes*.

纸	zhǐ	*paper*
笔	bǐ	*pen*
帽子	màozi	*hat*
鞋子	xiézi	*shoes*

Have you studied these characters enough to recognize them? Let's test them now. The following sentences all start with 我有 Wǒ yǒu (*I have . . .*) Only the object changes. What does each one mean?

1. 我有帽子。 _____

2. 我有笔。 _____

3. 我有鞋子。 _____

4. 我有纸。 _____

ANSWER KEY

1. Wǒ yǒu màozi. (*I have a hat.*) 2. Wǒ yǒu bǐ. (*I have a pen.*) 3. Wǒ yǒu xiézi. (*I have shoes.*) 4. Wǒ yǒu zhǐ.
(*I have paper.*)

Now read through Lesson Five: Stroke Order in your guide to characters. This
will complete the first part of the guide, and you'll know how to write the new
characters that you see.

Grammar Builder 1

▶ 5C Grammar Builder 1 (CD 2, Track 6)

The particle de 的 is placed after a pronoun or noun to change it into its
possessive form. Let's see how it works first with nouns.

the doctor	yīshēng	医生
the doctor's	yīshēng de	医生的
the doctor's shoes	yīshēng de xiézi	医生的鞋子
the nurse	hùshi	护士
the nurse's	hùshi de	护士的
the nurse's coat	hùshi de wàitào	护士的外套
the police officer	jǐngchá	警察
the police officer's	jǐngchá de	警察的
the police officer's hat	jǐngchá de màozi	警察的帽子

The particle de 的 works the same way with pronouns: wǒ 我 (*I*) becomes wǒ de
我的 (*my, mine*), nǐ 你 (*you*) becomes nǐ de 你的 (*your, yours*), etc.

my, mine	wǒ de	我的
our, ours	wǒmen de	我们的
your, yours	nǐ de	你的

Lesson 5: Descriptions, Adjectives, and Colors

your, yours (*plural*)	nǐmen de	你们的
his	tā de	他的
her, hers	tā de	她的
their, theirs	tāmen de	他们的

When acting as a possessive adjective (*my, your, our*), the phrases above are followed by the object.

our	wǒmen de	我们的
our camera	wǒmen de zhàoxiàngjī	我们的照相机
your (*plural*)	nǐmen de	你们的
your (*plural*) *paper*	nǐmen de zhǐ	你们的纸
her	tā de	她的
her hat	tā de màozi	她的帽子
their	tāmen de	他们的
their camera	tāmen de zhàoxiàngjī	他们的照相机

When acting as the possessive pronoun (*mine, yours, ours*), the phrase doesn't change form, but comes after the subject and verb shì 是 (*be*), just as in English.

ours	wǒmen de	我们的
The camera is ours.	Zhàoxiàngjī shì wǒmen de.	照相机是我们的。
yours (*plural*)	nǐmen de	你们的
The paper is yours.	Zhǐ shì nǐmen de.	纸是你们的。
hers	tā de	她的
The hat is hers.	Màozi shì tā de.	帽子是她的。
theirs	tāmen de	他们的
The camera is theirs.	Zhàoxiàngjī shì tāmén de.	照相机是他们的。

Ⅱ

At a Restaurant

At Work

Review Dialogues

Around Town

Everyday Life

Socializing

Vocabulary Builder 2

▶ 5D Vocabulary Builder 2 (CD 2, Track 7)

new	xīn	新
old (things)	jiù	旧
large, big	dà	大
small	xiǎo	小
good, fine	hǎo	好
bad	huài	坏
blue	lán	蓝
red	hóng	红
yellow	huáng	黄
green	lǜ	绿
black	hēi	黑
white	bái	白

⏸

✎ Vocabulary Practice 2

Fill in the blanks with the missing words, indicated in parentheses, and then translate the full sentence into English.

1. Qìchē _____. (*small*)

汽车小。

2. Màozi _____. (*black*)

帽子黑。

3. Bīnxiāng _____. (*old*)

冰箱旧。

4. Diànnǎo _____. (*new*)

电脑新。

5. Diànhuà _____. (*red*)

电话红。

ANSWER KEY

1. xiǎo (*The car is small.*) 2. hēi (*The hat is black.*) 3. jiù (*The refrigerator is old.*) 4. xīn (*The computer is new.*) 5. hóng (*The telephone is red.*)

Take It Further 2

Okay, you've learned some very useful descriptive terms. Let's focus on recognizing the characters for a few of them. *Big* and *small* should be easy to remember. 大 dà (*big*) looks like a person holding his hands out, to indicate that something is big. 小 xiǎo (*small*), on the other hand, looks like a person who's a bit dejected, with hands drooping at his sides!

大	dà	*large, big*
小	xiǎo	*small*

New and old are a bit trickier. 旧 jiù (*old*) looks a little like the number 18, as in, *old* enough to vote. 新 xīn (*new*) is more complicated, like when you're trying to figure out how to use a *new* remote control!

新	xīn	*new*
旧	jiù	*old*

Let's see if we can tackle a few of the colors now. Does 白 bái (*white*) remind you of a window, open to let some *white* light in? 黑 hēi (*black*) has something that might look like a window as well, with the diagonal strokes representing shades drawn, to keep the room dark. And if you look at 黄 huáng (*yellow*), you might be able to imagine the front of an approaching train, with a *yellow* headlight shining on you.

白	bái	*white*
黑	hēi	*black*
黄	huáng	*yellow*

For 蓝 lán (*blue*), imagine the four straight lines at the bottom as falling rain, which is water, which of course often looks *blue*. The simple vertical stroke at the right of 红 hóng (*red*) might remind you of a fire hydrant, which is often painted *red*. And can you see the backwards E at the top of 绿 lǜ? That's *ee* as in *green*.

蓝	lán	*blue*
红	hóng	*red*
绿	lǜ	*green*

There's a good chance that these suggested mnemonics make no sense at all to you! That's fine; but if that's so, try to come up with others that work. As you get into Part 2 of your *Guide to Chinese Characters*, you'll learn that there are radicals, or parts of characters, that give you a clue about the character's meaning. You've already come across the female radical 女 in 女人 nǚrén (*woman*) and 女孩 nǚhái (*girl*). We'll come back to others. For now, though, it will be helpful to know that Chinese characters often contain clues as to what they mean; it's not all abstract memorization! And learning to look at characters and come up with mnemonics, no matter how silly they are, is a great way to become familiar with basic characters until you're more familiar with the writing system.

Now that you've been distracted by that last paragraph, let's go back and see how many of those descriptive characters you remember! Give the pīnyīn and translation for each character below. Since we did so many this time, we'll add in some clues.

1. 旧 (*looks like 18*) _____

2. 绿 (*backwards capital E as in …*) _____

3. 小 *(drooping, dejected hands)* _____

4. 蓝 *(like falling rain)* _____

5. 白 *(open window, letting in light)* _____

6. 黑 *(shades drawn over the window)* _____

7. 新 *(complicated, like learning something ...)* _____

8. 黄 *(oncoming train, shining its light)* _____

9. 大 *(person with outstretched arms)* _____

10. 红 *(maybe a fire hydrant)* _____

ANSWER KEY

1. jiù (*old*); 2. lǜ (*green*); 3. xiǎo (*small*); 4. lán (*blue*); 5. bái (*white*); 6. hēi (*black*); 7. xīn (*new*); 8. huáng (*yellow*); 9. dà (*large, big*); 10. hóng (*red*)

Grammar Builder 2

▶ 5E Grammar Builder 2 (CD 2, Track 8)

To modify a noun with an adjective, simply place the adjective before the noun it modifies, just as in English.

(a) new coat	xīn wàitào	新外套
(an) old hat	jiù màozi	旧帽子
(a) large hat	dà màozi	大帽子
(a) good camera	hǎo zhàoxiàngjī	好照相机
(a) blue pen	lán bǐ	蓝笔
yellow paper	huáng zhǐ	黄纸
black shoes	hēi xiézi	黑鞋子

The particle de 的 is also used with adjectives. You can place it after the adjective, especially when the noun being described or modified is not there, for example after the verb shì 是 (*be*) in the pattern:

subject	shì 是	*adjective*	de 的

Compare the following pairs of sentences. In the first sentence of each pair, the full noun + adjective phrase is used, so there's no de 的 between lán and màozi. But the second sentence follows the pattern shown above, with only the adjective after shì 是 (*be*), so de 的 is used after lán.

My hat is a blue hat.	Wǒ de màozi shì lán màozi.	我的帽子是蓝帽子。
My hat is blue.	Wǒ de màozi shì lán de.	我的帽子是蓝的。
Your coat is a large coat.	Nǐ de wàitào shì dà wàitào.	你的外套是大外套。
Your coat is large.	Nǐ de wàitào shì dà de.	你的外套是大的。
The nurse's camera is a new camera.	Hùshi de zhàoxiàngjī shì xīn zhàoxiàngjī.	护士的照相机是新照相机。
The nurse's camera is new.	Hùshi de zhàoxiàngjī shì xīn de.	护士的照相机是新的。

Obviously using de 的 makes the sentence shorter. But the main reason for substituting the particle for the noun is that in Chinese adjectives are also used as verbs, such as the word hǎo 好 (*good, fine*) in the sentences you know very well:

Nǐ hǎo.
你好。
You are fine. (Hello.)

Wǒ hěn hǎo.
我很好。
I am very well.

Lesson 5: Descriptions, Adjectives, and Colors   85

Both are examples of an adjective being used as a verb. Therefore, to indicate that the adjective is *not* used as a verb but used as a modifier, it's necessary to put de 的 after it.

✎ Work Out 1

Let's do some listening comprehension, focusing on descriptive words and the construction with de 的 that you just learned. Listen to your audio, and fill in the missing words in the blanks provided.

▶ 5F Work Out 1 (CD 2, Track 9)

1. *My hat is new.*

   _____ màozi shì xīn de.

   我的帽子是新的。

2. *My black hat is new.*

   Wǒ de _____ màozi shì xīn de.

   我的黑帽子是新的。

3. *Your coat is old.*

   Nǐ de wàitào shì _____ de.

   你的外套是旧的。

4. *Your green coat is old.*

   Nǐ de _____ wàitào shì _____ de.

   你的绿外套是旧的。

5. *Her camera is good.*

   _____ zhàoxiàngjī shì _____ de.

   她的照相机是好的。

6. *Her large camera is good.*

   Tā de _____ zhàoxiàngjī shì _____ de.

   她的大照相机是好的。

7. *The paper is yours.*

   Zhǐ shì _____.

   纸是你们的。

8. *The red paper is yours.*

   _____ zhǐ shì _____ de.

   红纸是你们的。

9. *The pens are ours.*

   Bǐ shì _____.

   笔是我们的。

10. *The black pens are ours.*

   _____ bǐ shì wǒmen de.

   黑笔是我们的。

11. *The hats are theirs.*

   _____ shì tāmen de.

   帽子是他们的。

12. *The yellow hats are theirs.*

_____ màozi shì tāmen _____.

黄帽子是他们的。

ANSWER KEY

1. Wǒ de; 2. hēi; 3. jiǔ; 4. lù, jiǔ; 5. Tā de, hǎo; 6. dà, hǎo; 7. nǐmen de; 8. Hóng, nǐmen; 9. wǒmen de; 10. Hēi;
11. Màozi; 12. Huáng, de

Bring It All Together

▶ 5G Bring It All Together (CD 2, Track 10)

Let's put everything you've learned together in a few short sentences.

Tā de mǔqīn shì hǎo hùshi.
他的母亲是好护士。
His mother is a good nurse.

Hùshi de xiézi shì bái de.
护士的鞋子是白的。
The nurse's shoes are white.

Tā de tàitai shì hǎo jǐngchá.
他的太太是好警察。
His wife is a good police officer.

Jǐngchá de wàitào shì lán de.
警察的外套是蓝的。
The police officer's coat is blue.

✎ Work Out 2

A. Please unscramble the following sentences.

1. de/jǐngchá/màozi. 的/警察/帽子。 _____

   _____

2. bǐ/yīshēng/de. 笔/医生/的。 _____

   _____

3. xuésheng/de/xiézi. 学生/的/鞋子。 _____

   _____

4. zhàoxiàngjī/de/jiějie. 照相机/的/姐姐。 _____

   _____

B. Fill in the blank in each sentence below with the appropriate pīnyīn form of the word in parentheses.

1. Wǒ yǒu _____ wàitào. (green)

   我有绿外套。

2. Hùshi yǒu _____ xiézi. (red)

   护士有红鞋子。

3. Mèimei yǒu bái _____. (paper)

   妹妹有白纸。

4. Tāmen yǒu xīn _____. (hat)

   他们有新帽子。

C. Fill in the blank in each sentence below with the appropriate pīnyīn form of the word in parentheses.

1. Jǐngchá de xiézi shì _____ de. (black)

   警察的鞋子是黑的。

2. Nǐmen de _____ shì jiù de. (pen)

   你们的笔是旧的。

3. Yīshēng de zhàoxiàngjī shì _____ de. (new)

   医生的照相机是新的。

4. Lǎoshī de _____ shì huáng de. (coat)

   老师的外套是黄的。

ANSWER KEY
A. 1. Jǐngchá de màozi. 警察的帽子。 (The police officer's hat.) 2. Yīshēng de bǐ. 医生的笔。
(The doctor's pen.) 3. Xuésheng de xiézi. 学生的鞋子。 (The student's shoes.) 4. Jiějie de zhàoxiàngjī.
姐姐的照相机。 (The older sister's camera.)
B. 1. lǜ (I have a green coat.) 2. hóng (The nurse has red shoes.) 3. zhǐ (Younger sister has white paper.)
4. màozi (They have a new hat.)
C. 1. hēi (The police officer's shoes are black.) 2. bǐ (Your pen is old.) 3. xīn (The doctor's camera is new.)
4. wàitào (The teacher's coat is yellow.)

▶ 5H Work Out 2 (CD 2, Track 11)

   Now listen to your audio for some more audio-only practice

⏸

 Drive It Home

Let's practice adjectives, both with and without de. First, rewrite the model sentence by replacing the underlined adjective with each of the new adjectives in parentheses.

Hēi bǐ shì wǒ de. (bái, xīn, dà, lán, hóng, xiǎo)
The black pen is mine. (white, new, big, blue, red, small)

Now, let's modify the sentence slightly, so that we need de after the adjective. Again, rewrite the model sentence by replacing the underlined adjective with each of the new ones in parentheses.

Wǒ de bǐ shì hēi de. (bái, xīn, dà, lán, hóng, xiǎo)
My pen is black. (white, new, big, blue, red, small)

Parting Words

▶ 5I Parting Words (CD 2, Track 12)

Great work. Hěn hǎo. 很好。 Before we move on, you may want to know a few more words to do with clothing. You've already learned the words for *hat, shoes,* and *coat,* but here are some other words for yīfu 衣服 (*clothes*):

shirt	chènshān	衬衫
skirt	qúnzi	裙子
sweater	máoyī	毛衣

⏸

And that brings us to the end of Lesson Five. You learned:

☐ More basic vocabulary related to people and things.
   (Still unsure? Go back to 77.)

☐ How to express possession with the useful particle de 的.
   (Still unsure? Go back to 79.)

☐ Common adjectives, including colors.
   (Still unsure? Go back to 81.)

☐ How to use adjectives to describe people and things.
   (Still unsure? Go back to 84.)

☐ How to put it all together in a few simple sentences.
   (Still unsure? Go back to 88.)

Don't forget to practice and reinforce what you've learned by visiting **www.livinglanguage.com/languagelab** for flashcards, games, and quizzes for Lesson Five!

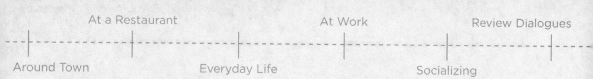
Word Recall

Match the English in the left column to the Chinese equivalent in the right.

1. *table*	a. màozi 帽子
2. *computer*	b. bǐ 笔
3. *chair*	c. shū 书
4. *telephone*	d. xiǎo 小
5. *book*	e. diànhuà 电话
6. *pen*	f. hùshi 护士
7. *hat*	g. huáng 黄
8. *camera*	h. lán 蓝
9. *police officer*	i. lǜ 绿
10. *coat*	j. yǐzi 椅子
11. *nurse*	k. huài 坏
12. *yellow*	l. wàitào 外套
13. *old*	m. xiézi 鞋子
14. *bad*	n. diànnǎo 电脑
15. *green*	o. zhàoxiàngjī 照相机
16. *small*	p. jǐngchá 警察
17. *shoes*	q. jiù 旧
18. *blue*	r. zhuōzi 桌子

ANSWER KEY

1. r; 2. n; 3.j; 4. e; 5. c; 6. b; 7. a; 8. o; 9. p; 10. l; 11. f; 12. g; 13. q; 14. k; 15. i; 16. d; 17. m; 18. h

Character Recall

Let's focus on the characters you've learned for things first. Match the characters in the right column with the pīnyīn in the left, and then give the translation.

1. 鞋子	a. zhuōzi
2. 电话	b. yǐzi
3. 纸	c. diànnǎo
4. 桌子	d. màozi
5. 书	e. xiézi
6. 电脑	f. zhǐ
7. 汽车	g. diànshì
8. 椅子	h. bǐ
9. 笔	i. diànhuà
10. 电视	j. qìchē
11. 帽子	k. shū

ANSWER KEY

1. e (shoes); 2. i (telephone); 3. f (paper); 4. a (table); 5. k (book); 6. c (computer); 7. j (car); 8. b (chair);
9. h (pen); 10. g (television); 11. d (hat)

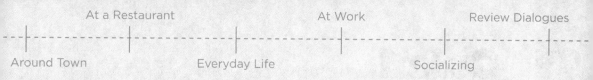
And now, let's do the same for descriptive words.

1. 黄	a. xīn
2. 白	b. dà
3. 大	c. jiù
4. 蓝	d. hēi
5. 新	e. lǜ
6. 黑	f. xiǎo
7. 旧	g. bái
8. 红	h. hóng
9. 小	i. huáng
10. 绿	j. lán

ANSWER KEY

1. i (*yellow*); 2. g (*white*); 3. b (*large, big*); 4. j (*blue*); 5. a (*new*); 6. d (*black*); 7. c (*old*); 8. h (*red*);
9. f (*small*); 10. e (*green*)

Lesson 5: Descriptions, Adjectives, and Colors   95

Quiz 1

Xiǎkǎo 1

小考 1

Now let's see how you've done so far. In this section you'll find a short quiz testing what you learned in Lessons 1–5. After you've answered all of the questions, score your quiz and see how you did! If you find that you need to go back and review, please do so before continuing on to Lesson 6.

You'll get a second quiz after Lesson 10, followed by a final review with five dialogues and comprehension questions. Let's get started!

A. Match the following Chinese words to the correct English translations:

1. shū 书	a. *to have*
2. gè 个	b. *very good*
3. yǒu 有	c. *large, big*
4. dà 大	d. *book*
5. hěn hǎo 很好	e. *(measure word for people, cities, groups, and nations)*

B. Translate the following English expressions into pīnyīn:

1. *Do you have an older sister?* _____

_____

2. *She has 15 students.* _____

_____

3. *I have two bicycles.* _____

_____

4. *The bookstore has ten women, three men.* _____

_____

5. *My mother is a good police officer.* _____

_____

C. Fill in the blanks with the correct measure word, and then translate the complete sentences into English.

1. Wǒ yǒu liǎng _____ shū.

2. Tā de mèimei yǒu sān _____ diànnǎo.

3. Wǒmen yǒu shíyī _____ yǐzi.

4. Qǐng gěi wǒ sì _____ píjiǔ.

5. Tāmen yǒu qī _____ qìchē.

D. Translate each possessive, and then give the meaning of the entire phrase in English.

1. *(the doctor's)* xiézi _____

2. *(our)* zhàoxiàngjī _____

3. *(the student's)* bǐ _____

4. *(the lawyer's)* zhuōzi _____

5. *(the laborer's)* màozi _____

E. Match the characters on the left to the pīnyīn on the right, and then give the translation.

1. 男人	a. hǎo
2. 好	b. xīn
3. 新	c. diànhuà

| 4. 六 | d. nánrén |
| 5. 电话 | e. liù |

How Did You Do?

Give yourself a point for every correct answer, then use the following key to
determine whether or not you're ready to move on:

0–10 points: It's probably best to go back and study the lessons again to make
sure you understood everything completely. Take your time; it's not a race!
Make sure you spend time reviewing the vocabulary and reading through each
Grammar Builder section carefully.

11–18 points: If the questions you missed were in sections A or B, you may want to
review the vocabulary from previous lessons again; if you missed answers mostly
in sections C or D, check the Grammar Builder sections to make sure you have
your grammar basics down. And if you had a hard time with section E, you should
go back and review your characters!

19–25 points: Feel free to move on to Lesson 6! You're doing a great job.

 **points**

Lesson 6: Around Town

Dì-liù kè: Fāngxiàng

第六课：方向

Welcome to Lesson Six. In this lesson, you'll learn your way around town, so you'll focus on:

- ☐ Key vocabulary related to locations around town.
- ☐ How to ask questions with nǎli 哪里 (*where*).
- ☐ More vocabulary for getting around.
- ☐ Expressing movement with qù 去 (*to go*) and location with zài 在 (*to be at*).
- ☐ Putting it all together in a short dialogue about asking for directions.

Vocabulary Builder 1

▶ 6B Vocabulary Builder 1 (CD 2, Track 14)

to be (located) at	zài	在
here	zhèlǐ	这里
there	nàli	那里
where	nǎli	哪里
(At) Where? Where is … ?	Zài nǎli?	在哪里？
post office	yóujú	邮局
theater	xìyuàn	戏院
restaurant	cānguǎn	餐馆
market	shìchǎng	市场
next to	pángbiān	旁边
left	zuǒ	左
on the left	zài zuǒbiān	在左边
right	yòu	右
on the right	zài yòubiān	在右边

⏸

✎ Vocabulary Practice 1

Match the English in the left column to the Chinese equivalent in the right.

1. left	a. shìchǎng 市场
2. restaurant	b. yòu 右
3. where	c. zài 在
4. market	d. zuǒ 左
5. to be (located) at	e. cānguǎn 餐馆
6. right	f. nǎli 哪里

ANSWER KEY
1. d; 2. e; 3. f; 4. a; 5. c; 6. b

Take It Further 1

Let's focus on a few characters related to some important places around town. Study each character, and try to come up with your own mnemonics that will help you remember each one.

邮局	yóujú	*post office*
戏院	xìyuàn	*theater*
餐馆	cānguǎn	*restaurant*
市场	shìchǎng	*market*

Ready? See if you can match the character to the pīnyīn, and then translate each answer.

1. 市场	a. xìyuàn
2. 戏院	b. yóujú
3. 邮局	c. shìchǎng
4. 餐馆	d. cānguǎn

ANSWER KEY
1. c (*market*); 2. a (*theater*); 3. b (*post office*); 4. d (*restaurant*)

Now read through the introduction to Part 2: Reading, as well as Lesson Six: Introduction to Radicals, in your guide to characters.

Since you've completed Part 1: Writing, you might consider going back over the Take It Further sections in earlier lessons so that you can practice writing out the characters you've learned to recognize. Don't worry if your characters don't look quite as good as the ones you see in this course book or in your *Guide to Chinese Characters*. It takes practice!

Grammar Builder 1

When you ask a question in Chinese with a question word such as nǎli 哪里 (*where*), it stays in the same place in the sentence as the answer. This is similar to English "echo" questions, those questions that you ask when you're not sure you heard an answer correctly:

A: The post office is next to the market.
B: Pardon? The post office is where?

The word order in B is the regular word order for questions in Chinese. Listen to your audio and take a look at these examples. Note that the position of the question word, nǎli 哪里 (*where*), is the same as the word or phrase that gives you the answer.

6C Grammar Builder 1 (CD 2, Track 15)

Where is the post office?	Yóujú zài nǎli?	邮局在哪里?
The post office is here.	Yóujú zài zhèlǐ.	邮局在这里。
Where is the market?	Shìchǎng zài nǎli?	市场在哪里?
The market is there.	Shìchǎng zài nàli.	市场在那里。
Where is the restaurant?	Cānguǎn zài nǎli?	餐馆在哪里?
The restaurant is on the left.	Cānguǎn zài zuǒbiān.	餐馆在左边。
The restaurant is next to the market.	Cānguǎn zài shìchǎng pángbiān.	餐馆在市场旁边。
Where is the theater?	Xìyuàn zài nǎli?	戏院在哪里?
The theater is on the right.	Xìyuàn zài yòubiān.	戏院在右边。
The theater is next to the post office.	Xìyuàn zài yóujú pángbiān.	戏院在邮局旁边。

Vocabulary Builder 2

▶ 6D Vocabulary Builder 2 (CD 2, Track 16)

east	dōng	东
west	xī	西
south	nán	南
north	běi	北
to go	qù	去
hotel	lǚguǎn	旅馆
hospital	yīyuàn	医院
restroom	cèsuǒ	厕所
police station	jǐngchá jú	警察局
bookstore	shūdiàn	书店
school	xuéxiào	学校

⏸

✎ Vocabulary Practice 2

Please fill in the blanks with missing syllables.

1. _____ yuàn *(hospital)*

2. xué _____ *(school)*

3. lǚ _____ *(hotel)*

4. jǐng _____ jú *(police station)*

5. shū _____ *(bookstore)*

6. _____ suǒ *(restroom)*

ANSWER KEY

1. yī; 2. xiào; 3. guǎn; 4. chá; 5. diàn; 6. cè

Take It Further 2

Let's focus on four more Chinese characters that will help you get around town. Study these, forming your own mnemonics to help you remember them. Notice that 医院 yīyuàn (*hospital*) and 戏院 xìyuàn (*theater*), which you learned in Take It Further 1, both end in 院 yuàn, which literally means courtyard or compound, but is generally found in words for public institutions.

厕所	cèsuǒ	*restroom*
旅馆	lǚguǎn	*hotel*
医院	yīyuàn	*hospital*
学校	xuéxiào	*school*

Have you familiarized yourself with these new characters? Great, let's review them, along with the four you learned earlier in this lesson. Match the characters with the pīnyīn, and then translate.

1. 旅馆	a. cānguǎn
2. 市场	b. xuéxiào
3. 邮局	c. shìchǎng
4. 学校	d. xìyuàn
5. 厕所	e. lǚguǎn
6. 餐馆	f. yīyuàn
7. 医院	g. cèsuǒ
8. 戏院	h. yóujú

ANSWER KEY

1. e (*hotel*); 2. c (*market*); 3. h (*post office*); 4. b (*school*); 5. g (*restroom*); 6. a (*restaurant*); 7. f (*hospital*); 8. d (*theater*)

Grammar Builder 2

 6E Grammar Builder 2 (CD 2, Track 17)

Zài 在 (*to be [located] at*) and qù 去 (*to go [to]*) are both verbs. Therefore, their sentence structures are the same when using the question word nǎli 哪里 (*where*) to ask where something is, or where someone is going. Notice that you don't need a preposition after the verb qù 去, which already carries the meaning of *to* in English.

Where are you going?	Nǐ qù nǎli?	你去哪里？
I am going [to] the hotel.	Wǒ qù lǚguǎn.	我去旅馆。
Where is the hotel?	Lǚguǎn zài nǎli?	旅馆在哪里？
The hotel is next to the post office.	Lǚguǎn zài yóujú pángbiān.	旅馆在邮局旁边。
Where is he going?	Tā qù nǎli?	他去哪里。
He is going [to] the hospital.	Tā qù yīyuàn.	他去医院。
Where is the hospital?	Yīyuàn zài nǎli?	医院在哪里？
The hospital is next to the school.	Yīyuàn zài xuéxiào pángbiān.	医院在学校旁边。
Where are we going?	Wǒmen qù nǎli?	我们去哪里？
We are going [to] the bookstore.	Wǒmen qù shūdiàn.	我们去书店。
Where is the bookstore?	Shūdiàn zài nǎli?	书店在哪里？
The bookstore is there.	Shūdiàn zài nàli.	书店在那里。

✎ Work Out 1

It's time for a listening comprehension work out. Fill in the blanks with the missing pīnyīn words or phrases.

▶ 6F Work Out 1 (CD 2, Track 18)

1. *Where is she going?*

   Tā qù _____?

   她去哪里？

2. *She is going to the police station.*

   Tā _____ jǐngchá jú.

   她去警察局。

3. *Where is the police station?*

   Jǐngchá jú _____?

   警察局在哪里？

4. *The police station is on the east side of the school.*

   _____ jú zài _____ dōng biān.

   警察局在学校东边。

5. *The police station is on the west side of the theater.*

   Jǐngchá jú _____ xìyuàn xī _____.

   警察局在戏院西边。

6. *Where are they going?*

   Tāmen _____?

   他们去哪里？

7. *They are going to the restroom.*

   Tāmen _____.

   他们去厕所。

8. *Where is the restroom?*

   Cèsuǒ _____ nǎli?

   厕所在哪里?

9. *The restroom is next to the market.*

   Cèsuǒ zài shìchǎng _____.

   厕所在市场旁边。

10. *The market is here.*

    Shìchǎng zài _____.

    市场在这里。

11. *The restroom is there.*

    Cèsuǒ _____.

    厕所在那里。

ANSWER KEY

1. nǎli; 2. qù; 3. zài nǎli; 4. Jǐngchá, xuéxiào; 5. zài, biān; 6. qù nǎli; 7. qù cèsuǒ; 8. zài; 9. pángbiān; 10. zhèlǐ; 11. zài nàli

Ⅱ

Essential Expressions

Numbers

Descriptions, Adjectives,
and Colors

People and Family

Around the Home

🔊 Bring It All Together

▶ 6G Bring It All Together (CD 2, Track 19)

Good job. Now listen to the following exchange.

Zhēn:	Nǐ qù nǎli? 你去哪里? *Where are you going?*
Lín:	Wǒ qù yóujú. 我去邮局。 *I am going to the post office.*
Zhēn:	Yóujú zài nǎli? 邮局在哪里? *Where is the post office?*
Lín:	Yóujú zài yīyuàn běi biān. 邮局在医院北边。 *The post office is north of the hospital.*
Zhēn:	Wǒmen qù nǎli? 我们去哪里? *Where are we going?*
Lín:	Wǒmen qù cānguǎn. 我们去餐馆。 *We are going to the restaurant.*
Zhēn:	Cānguǎn zài nǎli? 餐馆在哪里? *Where is the restaurant?*
Lín:	Cānguǎn zài lǚguǎn dōng biān. 餐馆在旅馆东边。 *The restaurant is on the east side of the hotel.*
Zhēn:	Dà yīyuàn zài nǎli? 大医院在哪里? *Where is the large hospital?*

Lín:	Dà yīyuàn zài xiǎo jǐngchá jú xī biān.
	大医院在小警察局西边。
	The large hospital is west of the small police station.
Zhēn:	Jǐngchá jú zài nǎli?
	警察局在哪里？
	Where is the police station?
Lín:	Jǐngchá jú zài zhèlǐ.
	警察局在这里。
	The police station is here.

Ⅱ

✎ Work Out 2

Translate the following sentences into English.

1. Cānguǎn zài nǎli? 餐馆在哪里？ _____

_____

2. Cānguǎn zài yòubiān. 餐馆在右边。 _____

_____

3. Yīyuàn zài nǎli? 医院在哪里？ _____

_____

4. Yīyuàn zài yóujú pángbiān. 医院在邮局旁边。 _____

_____

5. Tāmen qù nǎli? 他们去哪里？ _____

_____

6. Tāmen qù shìchǎng. 他们去市场。 _____

_____

7. Shìchǎng zài nǎli? 市场在哪里? _____

_____

8. Shìchǎng zài jǐngchá jú nán biān. 市场在警察局南边。 _____

_____

ANSWER KEY

1. *Where is the restaurant?* 2. *The restaurant is on the right.* 3. *Where is the hospital?* 4. *The hospital is next to the post office.* 5. *Where are they going?* 6. *They are going to the market.* 7. *Where is the market?* 8. *The market is south of the police station.*

▶ 6H Work Out 2 (CD 2, Track 20)

Now listen to your audio for additional audio-only practice.

⏸

✎ Drive It Home

Let's practice constructions with zài 在 (*to be located*) and qù 去 (*to go*). Answer each question in a full sentence using all of the phrases in parentheses. Speak aloud and write out each answer.

1. Cānguǎn zài nǎli? (zhèlǐ, nàli, zuǒbiān, yòubiān, shìchǎng pángbiān) *Where's the restaurant? (here, there, on the left, on the right, next to the market)* _____

_____

2. Lǚguǎn zài nǎli? (zhèli, nàli, zuǒbiān, yòubiān, cānguǎn pángbiān) *Where's the hotel? (here, there, on the left, on the right, next to the restaurant)* _____

_____

3. Nǐ qù nǎli? (lǚguǎn, yóujú, cānguǎn, yīyuàn) *Where are you going? (to the hotel, to the post office, to the restaurant, to the hospital)* _____

    _____

4. Wǒmen qù nǎli? (shūdiàn, xuéxiào, shìchǎng, lǚguǎn) *Where are we going? (to the bookstore, to the school, to the market, to the hotel)* _____

    _____

Parting Words

▶ 6I Parting Words (CD 2, Track 21)

Excellent. Fēicháng hǎo. 非常好。 Now you know how to use the question word nǎli 哪里 (*where*) and the verbs zài 在 (*to be located somewhere*) and qù 去 (*to go somewhere*). You also learned many words related to places and locations. Here are a few more you can add to what you already know:

university	dàxué	大学
pharmacy	yàofáng	药房
office	bàngōngshì	办公室
store	shāngdiàn	商店

⏸

And that brings us to the end of Lesson Six, which focused on:

☐ Key vocabulary related to locations around town.
   (Still unsure? Go back to 100.)

☐ How to ask questions with nǎli 哪里 (where).
   (Still unsure? Go back to 102.)

☐ More vocabulary for getting around.
   (Still unsure? Go back to 103.)

☐ Expressing movement with qù 去 (to go) and location with zài 在 (to be at).
   (Still unsure? Go back to 105.)

☐ Putting it all together in a short dialogue about asking for directions.
   (Still unsure? Go back to 108.)

Don't forget to practice and reinforce what you've learned by visiting **www.livinglanguage.com/languagelab** for flashcards, games, and quizzes for Lesson Six!

Word Recall

Match the English in the left column to the Chinese equivalent in the right.

1. *right*	a. yīshēng 医生
2. *where*	b. bái 白
3. *big*	c. shìchǎng 市场
4. *white*	d. zhǐ 纸
5. *new*	e. cānguǎn 餐馆
6. *to go*	f. nǎli 哪里
7. *to be (located) at*	g. pángbiān 旁边
8. *red*	h. dà 大
9. *left*	i. zuǒ 左
10. *paper*	j. qù 去
11. *restaurant*	k. yòu 右
12. *market*	l. xīn 新
13. *next to*	m. zài 在
14. *black*	n. hóng 红
15. *doctor*	o. hēi 黑

ANSWER KEY

1. k; 2. f; 3. h; 4. b; 5. l; 6. j; 7. m; 8. n; 9. i; 10. d; 11. e; 12. c; 13. g; 14. o; 15. a

Character Recall

Translate the following question-answer pairs from Chinese characters into pīnyīn and English. Each question contains a pronoun, which you learned back in Lessons 1 and 2, along with the verb qù 去 (*go*) and the question word nǎli 哪里 (*where*).

1. A. 你去哪里? _____

   B. 我去旅馆。 _____

2. A. 他去哪里? _____

   B. 他去学校。 _____

3. A. 她去哪里? _____

   B. 她去邮局。 _____

4. A. 他们去哪里? _____

   B. 他们去餐馆。 _____

5. A. 你们去哪里? _____

   B. 我们去市场。 _____

ANSWER KEY

1. A. Nǐ qù nǎli? (*Where are you going?*) B. Wǒ qù lǚguǎn. (*I'm going to the hotel?*) 2. A. Tā qù nǎli? (*Where is he going?*) B. Tā qù xuéxiào. (*He's going to the school.*) 3. A. Tā qù nǎli? (*Where is she going?*) B. Tā qù yóujú. (*She's going to the post office.*) 4. A. Tāmen qù nǎli? (*Where are they going?*) B. Tāmen qù cānguǎn. (*They're going to the restaurant.*) 5. A. Nǐmen qù nǎli? (*Where are you [pl.] going?*) B. Wǒmen qù shìchǎng. (*We're going to the market.*)

Lesson 7: At a Restaurant

Dì-qī kè: Cānguǎn
第七课: 餐馆

Welcome to Lesson Seven, which will give you a lot of new words, expressions, and grammar that you can take with you to a restaurant! In this lesson, you'll learn:

☐ Basic vocabulary for food and restaurants.

☐ How to ask questions with yǒu méi yǒu? 有没有? (*do you have?*).

☐ More vocabulary for food and restaurants.

☐ Polite requests and measure words related to food.

☐ How to put it all together in an exchange in a restaurant.

Vocabulary Builder 1

7B Vocabulary Builder 1 (CD 2, Track 23)

used to make an invitation or ask a favor	qǐng	请
to ask	wèn	问
May I ask?	qǐngwèn	请问
dish of food	cài	菜
to order food	diǎn cài	点菜
what	shénme	什么
what to order?	diǎn shénme cài?	点什么菜?
chicken	jī	鸡
roast	kǎo	烤
roast chicken	kǎo jī	烤鸡
duck	yā	鸭
Peking duck	Běijīng (kǎo) yā	北京(烤)鸭
fish	yú	鱼
steamed	qīng zhēng	清蒸
steamed fish	qīng zhēng yú	清蒸鱼
don't have	méi yǒu	没有
Do you have? (lit., have or don't have?)	Yǒu méi yǒu?	有没有?

✎ Vocabulary Practice 1

Match the English word in column A with its appropriate translation in column B.

1. *what*	a. méi yǒu 没有
2. *May I ask?*	b. diǎn cài 点菜
3. *don't have*	c. cài 菜
4. *dish of food*	d. shénme 什么
5. *to order food*	e. qǐngwèn 请问

ANSWER KEY
1. d; 2. e; 3. a; 4. c; 5. b

Take It Further 1

Let's focus on three characters that you're likely to see on a menu.

鸡	jī	*chicken*
鸭	yā	*duck*
鱼	yú	*fish*

Have you committed them to memory? Let's see. Give the pīnyīn and translation for each.

1. 鸡 _____

2. 鱼 _____

3. 鸭 _____

ANSWER KEY
1. jī (*chicken*); 2. yú (*fish*); 3. yā (*duck*)

Of course, you'll probably see types of preparation on a menu as well, so let's look at:

烤	kǎo	*roast*
清蒸	qīng zhēng	*steamed*

Now let's put them together. Could you identify these items on a menu? Give the pīnyīn and English for each one. Do you remember the third one?

1. 烤鸡 _____

2. 清蒸鱼 _____

3. 北京烤鸭 _____

ANSWER KEY
1. kǎo jī (*roast chicken*); 2. qīng zhēng yú (*steamed fish*); 3. Běijīng kǎo yā (*Peking duck*)

Now is a good time to cover Lesson 7 in your *Guide to Chinese Characters*.

Grammar Builder 1
▶ 7C Grammar Builder 1 (CD 2, Track 24)

Yǒu méi yǒu 有没有 literally means *have [or] don't have*. The word méi 没 is added to form the negative of yǒu 有. This structure of putting positive and negative forms together is the most common way to ask questions without using any question words. Let's practice this with the polite expression qǐngwèn 请问 (*May I ask?*).

May I ask, do you have steamed fish?
Qǐngwèn, nǐmen yǒu méi yǒu qīng zhēng yú?
请问，你们有没有清蒸鱼？

May I ask, do you have Peking duck?
Qǐngwèn, nǐmen yǒu méi yǒu Běijīng yā?
请问，你们有没有北京鸭？

May I ask, do you have roast chicken?
Qǐngwèn, nǐmen yǒu méi yǒu kǎo jī?
请问，你们有没有烤鸡？

You already know how to say you have something. To say you don't have something, you can say Wǒ méi yǒu ... 我没有 ... followed by what you don't have, or simply say Méi yǒu. 没有。

Vocabulary Builder 2

7D Vocabulary Builder 2 (CD 2, Track 25)

Let's learn more new words for food.

braised (in soy sauce)	hóng shāo	红烧
pork	zhūròu	猪肉
braised pork	hóng shāo zhūròu, hóng shāo ròu	红烧猪肉, 红烧肉
spare ribs	páigǔ	排骨
stir-fried	chǎo	炒
beef	niúròu	牛肉
vegetables	shūcài	蔬菜
sour	suān	酸
spicy	là	辣
soup	tāng	汤
wine, alcohol	jiǔ	酒
beer	píjiǔ	啤酒
tea	chá	茶
ice cream	bīngjilíng	冰激凌
to bring, to give	gěi	给
Please bring me ..., Please give me ...	Qǐng gěi wǒ ...	请给我 ...

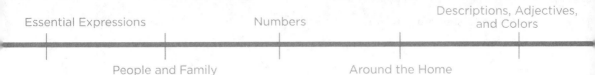
✎ Vocabulary Practice 2

Fill in the blanks with missing syllables.

1. pái _____ (*spare ribs*)

2. _____ jilíng (*ice cream*)

3. _____ cài (*vegetables*)

4. Qǐng gěi wǒ _____ jiǔ. (*Please give me beer.*)

5. Qǐng gěi wǒ _____. (*Please give me tea.*)

6. Qǐng gěi wǒ _____. (*Please give me soup.*)

ANSWER KEY
1. gǔ; 2. bīng; 3. shū; 4. pí; 5. chá; 6. tāng

Take It Further 2

Okay, now let's look at a few more characters that you're likely to see on a menu. Notice that the characters for *pork* and *beef* both include 肉 ròu (*meat*), along with the characters for 猪 zhū (*pig*) and 牛 niú (*cow, cattle*).

猪肉	zhūròu	*pork*
牛肉	niúròu	*beef*
蔬菜	shūcài	*vegetables*
茶	chá	*tea*
炒	chǎo	*stir-fried*

Have you committed those to memory? Are you ready to review all of the food-related characters you've learned in this lesson? Match the character on the left with the pīnyīn on the right, and then give the English translation.

1. 茶	a. kǎo
2. 鸭	b. chǎo

3. 蔬菜	c. yā
4. 炒	d. jī
5. 猪肉	e. yú
6. 鸡	f. shūcài
7. 烤	g. zhūròu
8. 牛肉	h. chá
9. 清蒸	i. niúròu
10. 鱼	j. qīng zhēng

ANSWER KEY

1. h (*tea*); 2. c (*duck*); 3. f (*vegetables*); 4. b (*stir-fried*); 5. g (*pork*); 6. d (*chicken*); 7. a (*roast*); 8. i (*beef*); 9. j (*steamed*); 10. e (*fish*)

Grammar Builder 2

Back in Vocabulary Builder 2 you learned the expression Qǐng gěi wǒ ... 请给我 ... (*Please bring/give me ...*). You can actually use any pronoun in place of wǒ 我 in this construction, which will be helpful when you're ordering food. Let's see some examples.

▶ 7E Grammar Builder 2 (CD 2, Track 26)

Please bring me ...	Qǐng gěi wǒ ...	请给我 ...
Please bring her ...	Qǐng gěi tā ...	请给她 ...
Please bring us ...	Qǐng gěi wǒmen ...	请给我们 ...
Please bring them ...	Qǐng gěi tāmen ...	请给他们 ...

And here are some measure words you'll need to know for ordering food:

| *bowl (for soup)* | wǎn | 碗 |
| *two soups, two bowls of soup* | liǎng wǎn tāng | 两碗汤 |

cup, glass (for water, coffee, tea, wine)	bēi	杯
three teas, three cups of tea	sān bēi chá	三杯茶
bottle (for bottled drinks)	píng	瓶
two beers, two bottles of beer	liǎng píng píjiǔ	两瓶啤酒
dish, plate (general unit for ordering food)	pán	盘
one chicken dish and one fish dish	yī pán jī, yī pán yú	一盘鸡,一盘鱼

Work Out 1

Let's use these measure words in complete sentences with the expression *Please bring me* ... Qǐng gěi wǒ ... Listen to your audio and fill in the blanks with the word or phrase that you hear.

▶ 7F Work Out 1 (CD 2, Track 27)

1. *Please bring us three vegetable soups.*

   _____ sān wǎn shūcài tāng.

   请给我们三碗蔬菜汤。

2. *Please bring her one spicy beef.*

   Qǐng gěi tā yī pán _____.

   请给她一盘辣牛肉。

3. *Please bring me one braised chicken, one roast duck.*

Qǐng gěi _____ yī _____ hóng shāo jī, yī pán _____.

请给我一盘红烧鸡，一盘烤鸭。

4. *Please bring us two teas, three beers.*

Qǐng gěi wǒmen _____ chá, _____ píjiǔ.

请给我们两杯茶，三瓶啤酒。

5. *Please bring them two red wines.*

Qǐng gěi tāmen liǎng bēi _____.

请给他们两杯红酒。

ANSWER KEY

1. Qǐng gěi wǒmen; 2. là niúròu; 3. wǒ, pán, kǎo yā; 4. liǎng bēi, sān píng; 5. hóngjiǔ

Bring It All Together

▶ 7G Bring It All Together (CD 2, Track 28)

Wáng:	Nǐmen de chá hěn hǎo.
	你们的茶很好。
	Your tea is very good.
Lán:	Xièxie.
	谢谢。
	Thank you.
	Nǐmen diǎn shénme cài?
	你们点什么菜？
	What would you like to order?
Wáng:	Nǐmen yǒu méiyǒu suān là tāng?
	你们有没有酸辣汤？

Do you have hot and sour soup?

Lán:　　Wǒmen méiyǒu suān là tāng.

我们没有酸辣汤。

We don't have hot and sour soup.

Yǒu shūcài jī tāng, páigǔ tāng.

有蔬菜鸡汤，排骨汤。

(We) have chicken vegetable soup, spare rib soup.

Wáng:　　Yǒu méiyǒu là de tāng?

有没有辣的汤？

Do you have spicy soup?

Lán:　　Là de niúròu tāng.

辣的牛肉汤。

Spicy beef soup.

Wáng:　　Qǐngwèn nǐmen yǒu shénme yú?

请问你们有什么鱼？

May I ask, what fish do you have?

Lán:　　Huáng yú hěn hǎo.

黄鱼很好。

Yellow fish is good.

Wǒmen yǒu qīng zhēng de, hóng shāo de.

我们有清蒸的，红烧的。

We have steamed and braised.

Wáng:　　Qǐngwèn yǒu méiyǒu hóng shāo niúròu?

请问有没有红烧牛肉？

May I ask, do you have braised beef?

Lán:　　Méiyǒu.

没有。

We don't.

Wǒmen yǒu hóng shāo zhūròu.

我们有红烧猪肉。

We have braised pork.

Wáng: Chǎo niúròu ne?

炒牛肉呢?

And stir-fried beef?

Lán: Yǒu.

有。

We do (have).

Wáng: Hǎo.

好。

Good.

Gěi wǒmen yī pán chǎo niúròu,

给我们一盘炒牛肉,

Bring us stir-fried beef,

yī pán Běijīng kǎo yā,

一盘北京烤鸭,

a Peking Duck,

yī pán qīng zhēng huáng yú,

一盘清蒸黄鱼,

a steamed yellow fish,

sān wǎn là niúròu tāng,

三碗辣牛肉汤,

three spicy beef soups,

yī píng píjiǔ.

一瓶啤酒。

one bottle of beer.

Gěi tā yī pán qīng zhēng páigǔ, yī bēi hóngjiǔ.

给她一个清蒸排骨,一杯红酒。

Bring her steamed spare ribs and a glass of red wine.

✎ Work Out 2

Now let's practice measure words. Fill in the missing measure words in each of the following, and then translate the complete sentence into English.

1. Gěi wǒmen yī _____ Běijīng kǎo yā.

_____

2. Qǐng gěi wǒ yī _____ tāng.

_____

3. Qǐng gěi wǒmen sān _____ píjiǔ.

_____

4. Qǐng gěi wǒmen liǎng _____ hóngjiǔ.

_____

5. Qǐng gěi wǒ yī _____ hóng shāo ròu.

_____

6. Qǐng gěi tā yī _____ jiǔ.

_____

7. Qǐng gěi wǒ sì _____ yú.

_____

8. Qǐng gěi wǒmen liù _____ jī tāng.

_____

ANSWER KEY

1. pán (*Bring us one Peking duck.*) 2. wǎn (*Please bring me a bowl of soup.*) 3. píng (*Please bring us three bottles of beer.*) 4. bēi (*Please bring us two glasses of red wine.*) 5. pán (*Please bring me a dish of braised pork.*) 6. píng (*Please bring him a bottle of wine.*) 7. pán (*Please bring me four dishes of fish.*) 8. wǎn (*Please bring us six bowls of chicken soup.*)

7H Work Out 2 (CD 2, Track 29)

Now listen to your audio for some additional audio-only practice.

✎ Drive It Home

Let's practice the expression you'll use to ask whether or not someone has something. Complete the question with all of the options supplied in parentheses, writing out and saying each full question aloud.

Yǒu méi yǒu … ? (qīng zhēng yú, Běijīng kǎo yā, kǎo jī, hóng shāo zhūròu, páigǔ, chǎo shūcài) *Do you have … ? (steamed fish, Peking duck, roast chicken, braised pork, spare ribs, stir fried vegetables)* _____

_____

Now, give the answers you might hear at a restaurant, both the affirmative with Wǒmen yǒu … , and the negative with Wǒmen méi yǒu … .

Parting Words

7I Parting Words (CD 2, Track 30)

Great. Hěn hǎo 很好。 Now you know how to order in Chinese restaurants, some words for food, the measure words for food items, and the polite expression qǐng 请. Here are a few more words that might be useful as you explore the wide world of Chinese cuisine:

xián	*salty*	咸
kǔ	*bitter*	苦
tián	*sweet*	甜

Have fun at the restaurant!

And that brings us to the end of Lesson Seven. By now, you should know:

☐ Basic vocabulary for food and restaurants.
(Still unsure? Go back to 116.)

☐ How to ask questions with yǒu méi yǒu 有没有 (*do you have?*).
(Still unsure? Go back to 118.)

☐ More vocabulary for food and restaurants.
(Still unsure? Go back to 119.)

☐ Polite requests and measure words related to food.
(Still unsure? Go back to 121.)

☐ How to put it all together in an exchange in a restaurant.
Still unsure? Go back to 123.)

Don't forget to practice and reinforce what you've learned by visiting **www.livinglanguage.com/ languagelab** for flashcards, games, and quizzes for Lesson Seven!

Word Recall

Match the English in the left column to the Chinese equivalent in the right.

1. *tea*	a. nàli 那里
2. *cup, glass (measure word for water, coffee, tea, wine)*	b. niúròu 牛肉
3. *to bring, to give*	c. píng 瓶
4. *dish, plate (measure word for a dish of food)*	d. bēi 杯
5. *stir-fried*	e. zhèlǐ 这里
6. *there*	f. pán 盘
7. *beef*	g. kǎo 烤
8. *(making an invitation or asking a favor)*	h. chá 茶
9. *wine, alcohol*	i. cèsuǒ 厕所
10. *hotel*	j. yóujú 邮局
11. *here*	k. chǎo 炒
12. *roast*	l. lǚguǎn 旅馆
13. *bottle (measure word for bottled drinks)*	m. jiǔ 酒
14. *vegetable*	n. qǐng 请
15. *restroom*	o. xìyuàn 戏院
16. *theater*	p. shūcài 蔬菜
17. *post office*	q. gěi 给

ANSWER KEY
1. h; 2. d; 3. q; 4.f; 5. k; 6. a; 7. b; 8. n; 9. m; 10. l; 11. e; 12. g; 13. c; 14. p; 15. i; 16. o; 17. j

Character Recall

Take a look at each line of characters below, and fill in the missing pīnyīn. Then, translate each full sentence. These sentences are all either identical, or very similar, to sentences that you read earlier in this lesson.

1. 你们的茶很好。

   _____ de _____ hěn hǎo.

2. 有蔬菜鸡汤。

   Yǒu _____ tāng.

3. 黄鱼很好。

   _____.

4. 我们有红烧猪肉。

   _____ yǒu hóng shāo _____.

5. 给我们一盘炒牛肉。

   Gěi _____ pán _____.

6. 给我们一盘北京烤鸭。

   Gěi _____ pán Běijīng _____.

ANSWER KEY

1. Nǐmen, chá (*Your tea is very good.*) 2. shūcài jī (*[We] have vegetable chicken soup.*) 3. Huáng yú hěn hǎo. (*[The] yellow fish is good.*) 4. Wǒmen, zhūròu (*We have braised pork.*) 5. wǒmen yī, chǎo niúròu (*Bring us one stir fried beef.*) 6. wǒmen yī, kǎo yā (*Bring us one Peking duck.*)

Lesson 8: Everyday Life

Dì-bā kè: Rìcháng shēnghuó

第八课: 日常生活

In this lesson, you'll learn:

☐ Time expressions like *morning*, *afternoon*, and *night*.

☐ How to tell time.

☐ Vocabulary for discussing your daily routine.

☐ How to ask *when* and *at what time*.

☐ How to put it all together in a short exchange about daily routines.

Vocabulary Builder 1

▶ 8B Vocabulary Builder 1 (CD 2, Track 32)

now	xiànzài	现在
How many?	jǐ	几
o'clock, hour	diǎn	点
o'clock, hour	diǎn zhōng	点钟
What time is it now?	Xiànzài jǐ diǎn?	现在几点?
What time is it now?	Xiànzài jǐ diǎn zhōng?	现在几点钟?
minute	fēn	分
three thirty (3:30)	sān diǎn sānshí fēn	三点三十分
to do, to make	zuò	做
to eat	chī	吃
breakfast	zǎocān	早餐
lunch	wǔcān	午餐
dinner	wǎncān	晚餐
morning	zǎoshang	早上
noon	zhōngwǔ	中午
afternoon	xiàwǔ	下午
evening, night	wǎnshang	晚上

⏸

✎ Vocabulary Practice 1

Match the English word in column A with its appropriate translation in column B.

1. *afternoon*	a. chī 吃
2. *breakfast*	b. wǎncān 晚餐
3. *o'clock, hour*	c. xiàwǔ 下午

| 4. *to eat* | d. zǎocān 早餐 |
| 5. *dinner* | e. diǎn 点 |

ANSWER KEY
1. c; 2. d; 3. e; 4. a; 5. b

Take It Further 1

Since you'll learn a few new important verbs in this lesson, let's focus on characters for verbs. You've already seen some of them in previous lessons.

是	shì	*to be*
有	yǒu	*to have*
在	zài	*to be (located) at*
去	qù	*to go*
做	zuò	*to do, to make*
吃	chī	*to eat*

Have you familiarized yourself with them? Let's add in a review of a few characters for pronouns and people. Translate the following subject-verb phrases into pīnyīn and English.

1. 我们吃 . . . _____

2. 女人去 . . . _____

3. 我做 . . . _____

4. 他们在 . . . _____

5. 男孩是 . . . _____

6. 她有 . . . _____

ANSWER KEY

1. wǒmen chī (*we eat . . .*); 2. nǚrén qù (the woman goes to . . .); 3. wǒ zuò (I do/make . . .); 4. tāmen zài (they are located at . . .); 5. nánhái shì (the boy is . . .); 6. tā yǒu (she has . . .)

Now is a good time to go over Lesson 8 in your *Guide to Chinese Characters.*

Grammar Builder 1

Remember that question words in Chinese appear in the same position in a sentence as their answer. In the following question-answer pairs, compare the position of the question word or phrase, for example jǐ diǎn 几点 (*what time*), to the position of the answer, for example bā diǎn 八点 (*at eight o'clock*).

8C Grammar Builder 1 (CD 3, Track 1)

What time does he eat breakfast?	Tā jǐ diǎn chī zǎocān?	他几点吃早餐?
He eats breakfast at eight.	Tā bā diǎn chī zǎocān.	他八点吃早餐。
What time is lunch?	Wǔcān shì jǐ diǎn?	午餐是几点?
Lunch is at 12 noon.	Wǔcān shì zhōngwǔ shí'èr diǎn.	午餐是中午十二点。
What time do you make lunch?	Nǐ jǐ diǎn zuò wǔcān?	你几点做午餐?
I make lunch at ten in the morning.	Wǒ zǎoshang shí diǎn zuò wǔcān.	我早上十点做午餐。
What time do you eat dinner?	Nǐ jǐ diǎn chī wǎncān?	你几点吃晚餐?
I eat dinner at seven in the evening.	Wǒ wǎnshang qī diǎn chī wǎncān.	我晚上七点吃晚餐。

Vocabulary Builder 2

▶ 8D Vocabulary Builder 2 (CD 3, Track 2)

time (in broad terms)	shíhou	时候
time (in hour and minutes)	shíjiān	时间
what time, when	shénme shíhou	什么时候
to teach	jiāo	教
to study, to learn	xué	学
Chinese	Zhōngwén	中文
English	Yīngwén	英文
to be at/go to work	shàngbān	上班
to be at/go to school	shàngxué	上学
to sleep	shuì	睡
to sleep	shuìjiào	睡觉

Ⅱ

✎ Vocabulary Practice 2

Fill in the blanks in the conversation below.

1. Nǐ shàng _____ ma? (*Do you go to school?*)

2. Wǒ _____ bān. Nǐ ne? (*I work. And you?*)

3. Wǒ xué _____ wén. (*I study Chinese.*)

4. Nǐ shénme shí _____ shàngxué? (*When do you go to school?*)

5. Wǒ _____ shang shàngxué. (*I go to school in the evening.*)

ANSWER KEY
1. xué; 2. shàng; 3. Zhōng; 4. hou; 5. wǎn

Take It Further 2

Let's go back and add a few more characters that we'll be able to practice in sentences with characters you've learned earlier. Notice that 学 xué (*to study, learn*) is also found in 学校 xuéxiào (*school*), which you learned in Lesson Six. If you look closely at 教 jiāo (*to teach*), you'll see that you can see a smaller version of the same radical in the lower lefthand corner. We'll also add the characters for languages, 中文 (*Chinese*) and 英文 (*English*), both of which contain 文 wén.

教	jiāo	to teach
学	xué	to study, to learn
上班	shàngbān	to be at work
中文	Zhōngwén	Chinese
英文	Yīngwén	English

Have you committed these new characters to memory? Let's test them, along with the other characters for verbs that you focused on in Take it Further 1. Match the Chinese character on the left to the pīnyīn on the right, and then translate into English.

1. 中文	a. chī
2. 吃	b. zài
3. 有	c. qù
4. 上班	d. shì
5. 去	e. zuò
6. 教	f. yǒu
7. 在	g. xué
8. 学	h. Zhōngwén
9. 是	i. Yīngwén
10. 英文	j. shàngbān
11. 做	k. jiāo

ANSWER KEY

1. h (*Chinese*); 2. a (*to eat*); 3. f (*to have*); 4. j (*to be at work*); 5. c (*to go*); 6. k (*to teach*); 7. b (*to be [located] at*); 8. g (*to study, to learn*); 9. d (*to be*); 10. i (*English*); 11. e (*to do, to make*)

Grammar Builder 2

▶ 8E Grammar Builder 2 (CD 3, Track 3)

When we ask about time, we can use either jǐ diǎn zhōng 几点钟 (*what hour, what time*) or shénme shíhou 什么时候 (*when*). Jǐ diǎn zhōng 几点钟 is used to ask specifically about the hour and the minutes, while shénme shíhou 什么时候 is more general. The answer can be a time of day, months or years. Let's hear this difference in the following dialogue.

A. What time is it?

Xiànzài jǐ diǎn zhōng?

现在几点钟?

B. Two twenty.

Liáng diǎn èrshí.

两点二十。

A. When do they study Chinese?

Tāmen shénme shíhou xué Zhōngwén?

他们什么时候学中文?

B. They study Chinese in the evening.

Tāmen wǎnshang xué Zhōngwén.

他们晚上学中文。

A. What time in the evening?

Wǎnshang jǐ diǎn zhōng?

晚上几点钟?

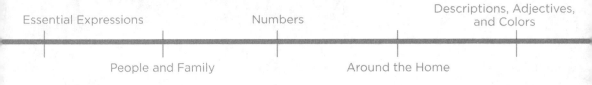
B. *Seven p.m.*
Wǎnshang qī diǎn.
晚上七点。

✎ Work Out 1

Now let's do some listening comprehension practice. Fill in the blanks in each sentence with the word or phrase you hear on your audio.

▶ 8F Work Out 1 (CD 3, Track 4)

1. *When do you all go to school?*

   Nǐmen shénme shíhou _____?

   你们什么时候上学?

2. *We go to school in the afternoon.*

   Wǒmen _____ shàngxué.

   我们下午上学。

3. *What time in the afternoon?*

   Xiàwǔ _____ zhōng?

   下午几点钟?

4. *Four p.m.*

   _____ sì _____.

   下午四点。

5. *When does she teach English?*

Tā _____ jiāo Yīngwén?

她什么时候教英文？

6. *She teaches English in the morning.*

Tā _____ jiāo Yīngwén.

她早上教英文。

7. *What time in the morning?*

Zǎoshang _____ ?

早上几点钟？

8. *Nine fifteen in the morning.*

Zǎoshang _____ diǎn shí _____ .

早上九点十五分。

9. *What time is breakfast?*

_____ shì jǐ diǎn zhōng?

早餐是几点钟？

10. *Breakfast is at eight forty.*

Zǎocān shì _____ sìshí.

早餐是八点四十。

11. *What time do you go to work?*

Nǐ jǐ diǎn zhōng _____ ?

你几点钟上班？

12. *I go to work at ten a.m.*

   Wǒ zǎoshang _____ shàngbān.

   我早上十点上班。

13. *What time do they make lunch?*

   Tāmen jǐ diǎn zhōng _____?

   他们几点钟做午餐?

14. *They make lunch at 12 noon.*

   Tāmen zhōngwǔ _____ zuò wǔcān.

   他们中午十二点做午餐。

15. *What time do you eat dinner?*

   Nǐ jǐ diǎn zhōng _____?

   你几点钟吃晚餐?

16. *I eat dinner at seven.*

   Wǒ _____ chī wǎncān.

   我七点吃晚餐。

17. *What time does he go to sleep?*

   Tā jǐ diǎn zhōng _____?

   他几点钟睡觉?

18. *He goes to sleep at 11 p.m.*

   Tā _____ shuìjiào.

   他晚上十一点睡觉。

ANSWER KEY

1. shàngxué; 2. xiàwǔ; 3. jǐ diǎn; 4. Xiàwǔ, diǎn; 5. shénme shíhou; 6. zǎoshang; 7. jǐ diǎn zhōng; 8. jiǔ, wǔ fēn; 9. Zǎocān; 10. bā diǎn; 11. shàngbān; 12. shí diǎn; 13. zuò wǔcān; 14. shí'èr diǎn; 15. chī wǎncān; 16. qī diǎn; 17. shuìjiào; 18. wǎnshang shíyī diǎn

🗨 Bring It All Together

▶ 8G Bring It All Together (CD 3, Track 5)

Let's listen to two people talking about their daily schedules.

Shān: Nǐmen shénme shíhou zuò wǔcān?

你们什么时候做午餐？

When do you make lunch?

Jìng: Wǒmen zhōngwǔ zuò wǔcān.

我们中午做午餐。

We make lunch at noon.

Shān: Nǐ mǔqīn jǐ diǎn zhōng jiāo Zhōngwén?

你母亲几点钟教中文？

What time does your mother teach Chinese?

Jìng: Tā xiàwǔ sān diǎn jiāo Zhōngwén.

她下午三点教中文。

She teaches Chinese at 3 p.m.

Shān: Nǐmen jǐ diǎn zhōng chī wǎncān?

你们几点钟吃晚餐？

What time do you eat dinner?

Jìng: Wǒmen xiànzài chī. Nǐ chī ma?

我们现在吃。你吃吗？

We are eating now. Would you like to eat?

✎ Work Out 2

Let's practice telling time. Answer the question Xiànzài jǐ diǎn? 现在几点?
(*What time is it now?*) by writing out the following answers in pīnyīn:

1. *1:00* _____

2. *3:30* _____

3. *5:20* _____

4. *7:45* _____

5. *9:10 in the morning* _____

6. *10:40 in the morning* _____

7. *6:30 in the evening* _____

ANSWER KEY
1. yī diǎn; 2. sān diǎn sānshí fēn; 3. wǔ diǎn èrshí fēn; 4. qī diǎn sìshíwǔ fēn; 5. zǎoshang jiǔ diǎn shí fēn;
6. zǎoshang shí diǎn sìshí fēn; 7. wǎnshang liù diǎn sānshí fēn

▶ 8H Work Out 2 (CD 3, Track 6)

Now listen to your audio for some more, audio-only practice.

⏸

✎ Drive It Home

Let's practice a few sentences with time expressions for some daily routines. Form sentences with the time phrase given in parentheses. Pay attention to where you place the time expression in Chinese.

1. Tā … chī zǎocān. (bā diǎn, jiǔ diǎn sānshí fēn, zǎoshang qī diǎn, shí diǎn èrshí fēn)

   He eats breakfast … (at eight, at 9:30, at seven in the morning, at 10:20) _____

   _____

2. Wǒmen … chī wǎncān. (wǎnshang qī diǎn, bā diǎn èrshí fēn, wǎnshang liùdiǎn

   sìshí fēn, qīdiǎn shíwǔ fēn) *We eat dinner … (at seven in the evening, at 8:20, at*

   6:40 in the evening, at 7:15) _____

   _____

3. Tāmen … xué Zhōngwén. (wǎnshang, xiàwǔ, zhōngwǔ, zǎoshang) *They study*

   Chinese … (in the evening, in the afternoon, at noon, in the morning) _____

   _____

Parting Words

▶ 8I Parting Words (CD 3, Track 7)

That was great. Fēicháng hǎo. 非常好。 The question word you just used: shénme 什么 (*what*), which you first learned when you learned about ordering food: diǎn shénme cài 点什么菜 (*what dish to order?*), is the most general question word. The term shénme rén 什么人 (*what person*) is used the same way as shéi 谁 (*who*). And shénme dìfang 什么地方 (*what place*) is used the same way as nǎli 哪里 (*where*).

You also learned the words Zhōngwén 中文 (*Chinese*) and Yīngwén 英文 (*English*).
Here are some other languages you may or may not already speak as well:

Yìdàlìwén	*Italian*	意大利文
Fǎwén	*French*	法文
Déwén	*German*	德文
Xībānyáwén	*Spanish*	西班牙文
Rìwén	*Japanese*	日文
Éwén	*Russian*	俄文

And that brings us to the end of Lesson Eight. By now you should know:

☐ Time expressions like *morning, afternoon,* and *night*.
  (Still unsure? Go back to 132.)

☐ How to tell time.
  (Still unsure? Go back to 134.)

☐ Vocabulary for discussing your daily routine.
  (Still unsure? Go back to 135.)

☐ How to ask *when* and *at what time*.
  (Still unsure? Go back to 137.)

☐ How to put it all together in a short exchange about daily routines.
  (Still unsure? Go back to 141.)

Don't forget to practice and reinforce what you've
learned by visiting **www.livinglanguage.com/
languagelab** for flashcards, games, and quizzes for
Lesson Eight!

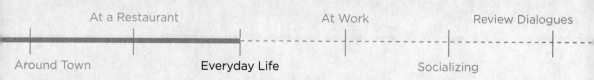
Word Recall

Match the English in the left column to the Chinese equivalent in the right.

1. *how many*	a. shénme 什么
2. *next to*	b. yòu 右
3. *May I ask?*	c. xiànzài 现在
4. *don't have*	d. zǎoshang 早上
5. *to be (located) at*	e. pángbiān 旁边
6. *noon*	f. chī 吃
7. *left*	g. diǎn cài 点菜
8. *used to make an invitation or ask a favor*	h. jǐ 几
9. *morning*	i. zài 在
10. *what*	j. qǐngwèn 请问
11. *to eat*	k. fēn 分
12. *to do, to make*	l. zhōngwǔ 中午
13. *(At) Where? Where is … ?*	m. xiàwǔ 下午
14. *now*	n. zuǒ 左
15. *to order food*	o. wǎnshang 晚上
16. *minute*	p. méi yǒu 没有
17. *evening, night*	q. zuò 做
18. *right*	r. Zài nǎli? 在哪里?

ANSWER KEY

1. h; 2. e; 3. j; 4. p; 5. i; 6. l; 7. n; 8. j; 9. d; 10. a; 11. f ; 12. q; 13. r; 14. c; 15. g; 16. k; 17. o; 18. b

Character Recall

Let's put a lot of the characters you've learned over the past several lessons to use in a few simple sentences. Look for characters for people, pronouns, verbs, food, objects, colors, and other descriptive words in the following. You've seen all of these characters before in the Take It Further sections.

1. 我们吃蔬菜。_____

2. 男人吃鱼。_____

3. 女人去市场。_____

4. 女孩去学校。_____

5. 男孩有蓝笔。_____

6. 她有小鞋子。_____

7. 他们学中文。_____

8. 她教英文。_____

ANSWER KEY

1. Wǒmen chī shūcài. (*We eat vegetables.*) 2. Nánrén chī yú. (*The man eats fish.*) 3. Nǚrén qù shìchǎng. (*The woman goes to the market.*) 4. Nǚhái qù xuéxiào. (*The girl goes to school.*) 5. Nánhái yǒu lán bǐ. (*The boy has a blue pen.*) 6. Tā yǒu xiǎo xiézi. (*She has small shoes.*) 7. Tāmen xué Zhōngwén. (*They study Chinese.*) 8. Tā jiāo Yīngwén. (*She teaches English.*)

Lesson 9: At Work

Dì-jiǔ kè: Zhíyè

第九课: 职业

In this lesson, you'll learn:

☐ Vocabulary for jobs and professions.

☐ How to ask about and express occupations.

☐ Days of the week and more expressions for telling time.

☐ More on using time expressions in sentences.

☐ How to put it all together in a conversation about work.

Vocabulary Builder 1

▶ 9B Vocabulary Builder 1 (CD 3, Track 9)

work, job, profession	gōngzuò	工作
what kind of work	shénme gōngzuò	什么工作
accounting	kuàijì	会计
accountant	kuàijìshī	会计师
engineering	gōngchéng	工程
engineer	gōngchéngshī	工程师
law	fǎlǜ	法律
lawyer	lǜshī	律师
laborer, worker	gōngrén	工人
store clerk	shòuhuòyuán	售货员

Ⅱ

✎ Vocabulary Practice 1

Fill in the table with the pīnyīn words or the English translations.

1.	what kind of work
2. gōngzuò	
3.	accountant
4.	engineer
5. gōngrén	
6. fǎlǜ	
7.	lawyer
8.	store clerk

ANSWER KEY

1. shénme gōngzuò; 2. *work, job, profession*; 3. kuàijìshī; 4. gōngchéngshī; 5. *laborer, worker*; 6. *law*;
7. lǜshī; 8. shòuhuòyuán

Take It Further 1

Let's take a closer look at a few key characters there. Notice how often gōng 工 appears in the following list. Also, can you pick out the single and double person radicals in any of these characters?

工作	gōngzuò	*work, job, profession*
什么工作	shénme gōngzuò	*what kind of work*
工程师	gōngchéngshī	*engineer*
工人	gōngrén	*laborer, worker*
律师	lùshī	*lawyer*

Have you familiarized yourself with these new characters? Let's review them. Do you remember your verbs zuò 做 (*to do, to make*) and shì 是 (*to be*)? Can you figure out that first question, and then identify the occupations in the answers?

1. 你做什么工作? _____

2. 我是律师。 _____

3. 我是工人。 _____

4. 我是工程师。 _____

ANSWER KEY

1. Nǐ zuò shénme gōngzuò? (*What kind of work do you do?*) 2. Wǒ shì lùshī. (*I'm a lawyer.*) 3. Wǒ shì gōngrén. (*I'm a laborer.*) 4. Wǒ shì gōngchéngshī. (*I'm an engineer.*)

Before you go on, take a look at Lessons 9 and 10 of your *Guide to Chinese Characters* to learn some more key radicals.

Grammar Builder 1

To ask what kind of work someone does, use the verb zuò 做 (*to do, to make*) along with the question phrase shénme gōngzuò 什么工作 (*what kind of work*). You can answer with the verb zuò 做 (*to do, to make*) or the verb shì 是 (*to be*), much as in English. Listen to your audio for some examples.

9C Grammar Builder 1 (CD 3, Track 10)

What work do you do?	Nǐ zuò shénme gōngzuò?	你做什么工作?
I do accounting.	Wǒ zuò kuàijì.	我做会计。
I am an accountant.	Wǒ shì kuàijìshī.	我是会计师。
What does she do?	Tā zuò shénme gōngzuò?	她做什么工作?
She does engineering.	Tā zuò gōngchéng.	她做工程。
She is an engineer.	Tā shì gōngchéngshī.	她是工程师。
What do you (pl.) do?	Nǐmen zuò shénme gōngzuò?	你们做什么工作?
She is a lawyer.	Tā shì lǜshī.	她是律师。
They are store clerks.	Tāmen shì shòuhuòyuán.	他们是售货员。
I am a laborer.	Wǒ shì gōngrén.	我是工人。

A brief note: The formal word for profession in Chinese is zhíyè 职业. But the question Nǐ de zhíyè shì shénme? 你的职业是什么? (*What is your profession?*) almost exclusively appears in writing and on questionnaires.

Vocabulary Builder 2

▶ 9D Vocabulary Builder 2 (CD 3, Track 11)

week	xīngqī	星期
Monday	xīngqī yī	星期一
Tuesday	xīngqī èr	星期二
Wednesday	xīngqī sān	星期三
Thursday	xīngqī sì	星期四
Friday	xīngqī wǔ	星期五
Saturday	xīngqī liù	星期六
Sunday	xīngqī tiān	星期天
day	tiān	天
which day	nǎ tiān	哪天
every day	měi tiān	每天
quarter of an hour (15 minutes)	kè	刻
quarter past eight	bā diǎn yī kè	八点一刻
half	bàn	半
half past four	sì diǎn bàn	四点半

Ⅱ

✎ Vocabulary Practice 2

1. xīng _____ liù *(Saturday)*

2. _____ tiān *(every day)*

3. xīngqī _____ *(Tuesday)*

4. nǎ_____ *(which day)*

5. _____ qī tiān *(Sunday)*

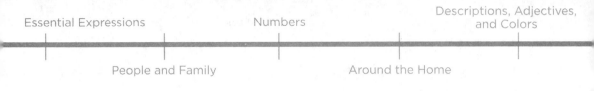

ANSWER KEY
1. qī; 2. měi; 3. èr; 4. tiān; 5. xīng

Take It Further 2

Now let's focus on the characters for the days of the week. You'll be happy to notice that they're quite easy. They're made up of the characters 星期 xīngqī (*week*) and the numbers, starting with Monday at number 1 一. Sunday uses the character 天 (*day*) instead of a number. Those are really the only three new characters involved. Take a look.

天	tiān	*day*
星期	xīngqī	*week*
星期一	xīngqī yī	*Monday*
星期二	xīngqī èr	*Tuesday*
星期三	xīngqī sān	*Wednesday*
星期四	xīngqī sì	*Thursday*
星期五	xīngqī wǔ	*Friday*
星期六	xīngqī liù	*Saturday*
星期天	xīngqī tiān	*Sunday*

Let's practice them. Give the pīnyīn and translation for each of the following.

1. 星期三	a. xīngqī tiān
2. 星期五	b. xīngqī liù
3. 星期一	c. xīngqī yī
4. 星期天	d. xīngqī sān
5. 星期四	e. xīngqī èr
6. 星期二	f. xīngqī wǔ
7. 星期六	g. xīngqī sì

ANSWER KEY
1. d (*Wednesday*); 2. f (*Friday*); 3. c (*Monday*); 4. a (*Sunday*); 5. g (*Thursday*); 6. e (*Tuesday*); 7. b (*Saturday*)

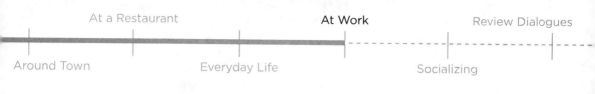
Grammar Builder 2

9E Grammar Builder 2 (CD 3, Track 12)

In Lesson 8, you learned that the time phrase comes before the verb in any statement or question. The full word order for the time phrase including days of the week is this:

Day (Monday)	>then>	Period of Day (morning, evening)	>then>	Time (hour, minutes, seconds)

Let's work on this.

Monday morning at 8 a.m.	Xīngqī yī zǎoshang bā diǎn.	星期一早上八点。
Tuesday morning 10 a.m.	Xīngqī èr zǎoshang shí diǎn.	星期二早上十点。
Wednesday afternoon at quarter past one.	Xīngqī sān xiàwǔ yī diǎn yī kè.	星期三下午一点一刻。
Thursday afternoon at 3:20 p.m.	Xīngqī sì xiàwǔ sān diǎn èrshí.	星期四下午三点二十。
Friday afternoon at 5 p.m.	Xīngqī wǔ xiàwǔ wǔ diǎn.	星期五下午五点。
Saturday evening at quarter past eight.	Xīngqī liù wǎnshang bā diǎn yī kè.	星期六晚上八点一刻。
Sunday evening at 11:40 p.m.	Xīngqī tiān wǎnshang shíyī diǎn sìshí.	星期天晚上十一点四十。
Every morning at half past nine.	Měi tiān zǎoshang jiǔ diǎn bàn.	每天早上九点半。

Essential Expressions

Numbers

Descriptions, Adjectives,
and Colors

People and Family

Around the Home

✎ Work Out 1

Let's do some listening comprehension practice. Listen to this short conversation, and fill in the blanks with the words or phrases that you hear on your audio.

▶ 9F Work Out 1 (CD 3, Track 13)

1. *Which day do you work?*

   Nǐ nǎ _____ shàng bān?

   你哪天上班?

2. *I work on Monday.*

   Wǒ _____ shàng bān.

   我星期一上班。

3. *Which day does the accountant go to work?*

   _____ nǎ tiān shàng bān?

   会计师哪天上班?

4. *The accountant works on every Wednesday.*

   Kuàijì shī měi _____ shàng bān.

   会计师每星期三上班。

5. *Which days does the lawyer go to work?*

   Lǜshī _____ tiān shàng bān?

   律师哪天上班。

6. *The lawyer works on Thursday and Friday.*

   Lǜshī _____, xīngqī wǔ shàng bān.

   律师星期四星期五上班。

7. *When do they go to work?*

Tāmen _____ shíhou shàng bān?

他们什么时候上班？

8. *The laborers go to work every morning at seven.*

Gōngrén _____ zǎoshang qī diǎn shàng bān.

工人每天早上七点上班。

9. *The store clerks work on Saturday and Sunday.*

_____ xīngqī liù, xīngqī tiān shàng bān.

售货员星期六，星期天上班。

ANSWER KEY

1. tiān; 2. xīngqī yī; 3. Kuàijìshī; 4. xīngqī sān; 5. nǎ; 6. xīngqī sì; 7. shénme; 8. měi tiān;
9. Shòuhuòyuán

Bring It All Together
9G Bring It All Together (CD 3, Track 14)

Zhāng: Nǐ zuò shénme gōngzuò?

你做什么工作？

What work do you do?

Lǐ: Wǒ shì shòuhuòyuán. Nǐ ne?

我是售货员。你呢？

I'm a store clerk. And you?

Zhāng: Wǒ xīngqī wǔ, xīngqī tiān zuò kuàijì.

我星期五，星期天做会计。

I work as an accountant on Fridays and Sundays.

Lǐ:	Nǐ xīngqī liù zuò shénme?
	你星期六做什么？
	What do you do on Saturdays?
Zhāng:	Wǒ shàng xué.
	我上学。
	I go to school.

✎ Work Out 2

Please unscramble the following sentences.

1. wǎnshang/xīngqī tiān/wǒ/chī yú. *(I eat fish on Sunday night.)* _____

   _____

2. qù/měi tiān/dìdi/shūdiàn/liǎng diǎn. *(Younger brother goes to the bookstore at two

   every day.)* _____

   _____

3. xīngqī yī/nǐmen/jiǔ diǎn/shàng bān/zǎoshang. *(You go to work on Monday

   morning at 9 am.)* _____

   _____

4. shìchǎng/zhōngwǔ/xīngqī wǔ/qù/tā. *(He goes to the market on Friday at noon.)*

   _____

   _____

5. shí diǎn bàn/xīngqī sān/wǎnshang/shuìjiào/wǒmen. *(We go to sleep on Wednesday

   night at half past ten.)* _____

   _____

ANSWER KEY

1. Wǒ xīngqī tiān wǎnshang chī yú. **2.** Dìdi měi tiān liǎng diǎn qù shūdiàn. **3.** Nǐmen xīngqī yī zǎoshang jiǔ diǎn shàng bān. **4.** Tā xīngqī wǔ zhōngwǔ qù shìchǎng. **5.** Wǒmen xīngqī sān wǎnshang shí diǎn bàn shuìjiào.

▶ 9H Work Out 2 (CD 3, Track 15)

Now, listen to your audio for some more practice and review.

Ⅱ

✎ Drive It Home

Let's do some more practice with time expressions. Rewrite each sentence below with each of the time expressions given in parentheses. Translate your answers into English.

1. Kuàijìshī … shàng bān. (xīngqī yī, měi xīngqī sān, měi tiān zǎoshang qī diǎn) _____

_____

2. Shòuhuòyuán … chī wǔcān. (xiàwǔ sān diǎn, xīngqī èr xiàwǔ, měi tiān zhōngwǔ)

_____

_____

3. Lǜshī … xué Yīngwén. (xīngqī wǔ zǎoshang, měi xīngqī sì wǎnshang bā diǎn, xīngqī

wǔ xiàwǔ yī diǎn bàn) _____

_____

ANSWER KEY

1. *The accountant works on Mondays/every Wednesday/every morning at 7.* **2.** *The store clerk eats lunch at three in the afternoon/on Tuesday afternoon/every day at noon.* **3.** *The lawyer studies English on Friday morning/every Thursday at 8 in the evening/Friday afternoon at half past one.*

Parting Words

 91 Parting Words (CD 3, Track 16)

Excellent. Fēicháng hǎo. 非常好. You did a lot of work just to learn about how to talk about work! You also learned five major question words and phrases:

shéi	*who*	谁
nǎli	*where*	哪里
shénme	*what*	什么
jǐ diǎn	*what time, when*	几点
nǎ tiān	*which day*	哪天

When telling time, there is another unit: seconds, and the word for it is miǎo 秒. So ten seconds would be shí miǎo 十秒, twenty seconds is èrshí miǎo 二十秒, and one minute and a half is yī fēn sānshí miǎo 一分三十秒 or yī fēn bàn 一分半。

And that brings us to the end of Lesson Nine. Which means that you should know:

☐ Vocabulary for jobs and professions. (Still unsure? Go back to 148.)

☐ How to ask about and express occupations. (Still unsure? Go back to 150.)

☐ Days of the week and more expressions for telling time. (Still unsure? Go back to 151.)

☐ More on using time expressions in sentences. (Still unsure? Go back to 153.)

☐ How to put it all together in a conversation about work.
(Still unsure? Go back to 155.)

Don't forget to practice and reinforce what you've learned by visiting **www.livinglanguage.com/languagelab** for flashcards, games, and quizzes for Lesson Nine!

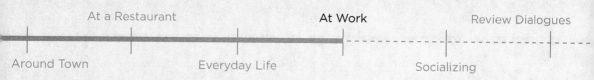
Word Recall

Match the English in the left column to the Chinese equivalent on the right.

1. *Do you have? (lit., have or don't have?)*	a. qīng zhēng 清蒸
2. *engineer*	b. wǎncān 晚餐
3. *duck*	c. kuàijì 会计
4. *law*	d. jī 鸡
5. *accounting*	e. xīngqī 星期
6. *steamed*	f. xīngqī liù 星期六
7. *Saturday*	g. diǎn zhōng 点钟
8. *dinner*	h. měi tiān 每天
9. *every day*	i. xīngqī tiān 星期天
10. *chicken*	j. gōngchéngshī 工程师
11. *laborer, worker*	k. yā 鸭
12. *breakfast*	l. bàn 半
13. *fish*	m. Yǒu méi yǒu? 有没有?
14. *Sunday*	n. nǎ tiān 哪天
15. *o'clock, hour*	o. gōngrén 工人
16. *week*	p. yú 鱼
17. *which day*	q. fǎlǜ 法律
18. *half*	r. zǎocān 早餐

ANSWER KEY

1. m; 2. j; 3. k; 4. q; 5. c; 6. a; 7. f; 8. b; 9. h; 10. d; 11. o; 12. r; 13. p; 14. i; 15. g; 16. e; 17. n; 18. l

Character Recall

Let's review the characters you learned in this lesson as well as some of the ones you learned earlier. Translate the following sentences into pīnyīn and English.

1. 你做什么工作? _____

    _____

2. 我是工人。 _____

    _____

3. 我教英文。 _____

    _____

4. 她做什么工作? _____

    _____

5. 她是工程师。 _____

    _____

6. 她是律师。 _____

    _____

ANSWER KEY
1. Nǐ zuò shénme gōngzuò? (*What kind of work do you do?*) 2. Wǒ shì gōngrén. (*I'm a laborer.*) 3. Wǒ jiāo Yīngwén. (*I teach English.*) 4. Tā zuò shénme gōngzuò? (*What kind of work does she do?*) 5. Tā shì gōngchéngshī. (*She's an engineer.*) 6. Tā shì lǜshī. (*She is a lawyer.*)

Lesson 10: Socializing

Dì-shí kè: Shèjiāo

第十课: 社交

Welcome to your last lesson of *Essential Chinese*. In this lesson, we'll focus on how people spend their free time. That means you'll learn:

☐ Essential vocabulary for talking about hobbies and free time.

☐ How to express likes and dislikes.

☐ Essential vocabulary for talking about sports and recreational activities.

☐ How to ask others about their hobbies and pastimes.

☐ How to put it all together in a short conversation about free time.

Vocabulary Builder 1

▶ 10B Vocabulary Builder 1 (CD 3, Track 18)

to like	xǐhuan	喜欢
to watch, to read silently	kàn	看
movies	diànyǐng	电影
newspaper	bàozhǐ	报纸
novel	xiǎoshuō	小说
to listen	tīng	听
music	yīnyuè	音乐
to drink	hē	喝
coffee	kāfēi	咖啡
no, not	bù	不
to not like	bù xǐhuan	不喜欢

Ⅱ

✎ Vocabulary Practice 1

Fill in the blanks with missing syllables.

1. yīn _____ (music)

2. _____ fēi (coffee)

3. xǐ _____ (to like)

4. xiǎo _____ (novel)

5. _____ yǐng (movies)

ANSWER KEY
1. yuè; 2. kā; 3. huan; 4. shuō; 5. diàn

Take It Further 1

Let's focus on a few characters that we'll be able to practice in sentences about likes and dislikes. Study these:

不	bù	*no, not*
喜欢	xǐhuan	*to like*
看	kàn	*to watch, to read silently*
听	tīng	*to listen*
喝	hē	*to drink*
音乐	yīnyuè	*music*
咖啡	kāfēi	*coffee*

Before we put them to use in some sentences, let's see if you can match the character on the left with the pīnyīn on the right. Then translate your answers.

1. 看	a. bù
2. 咖啡	b. kàn
3. 不	c. hē
4. 听	d. kāfēi
5. 喜欢	e. yīnyuè
6. 音乐	f. xǐhuan
7. 喝	g. tīng

ANSWER KEY

1. b (*to watch, to read silently*); 2. d (*coffee*); 3. a (*no, not*); 4. g (*to listen*); 5. f (*to like*); 6. e (*music*); 7. c (*to drink*)

Great. Now, let's try just a few quick sentences. Translate the following into pīnyīn and English.

1. 她喜欢音乐。 _____

2. 他喜欢喝咖啡。 _____

3. 女孩不喜欢看书。 _____

ANSWER KEY

1. Tā xǐhuan yīnyuè. (*She likes music.*) 2. Tā xǐhuan hē kāfēi. (*He likes to drink coffee.*) 3. Nǚhái bù xǐhuan kàn shū. (*The girl doesn't like to read books.*)

And now, in your last lesson of *Essential Chinese*, you're ready to turn to Lessons 11 and 12 of your *Guide to Chinese Characters* for some more information on radicals, as well as some practice.

Grammar Builder 1

▶ 10C Grammar Builder 1 (CD 3, Track 19)

The verb xǐhuan 喜欢 (*to like*) and its negative form bù xǐhuān 不喜欢 (*to not like*) can directly be followed by a noun such as kāfēi 咖啡 (*coffee*) or a verb phrase such as kàn diànyǐng 看电影 (*to watch movies*). No changes in the nouns or verbs are necessary. Let's listen to some examples.

She likes music.	Tā xǐhuan yīnyuè.	她喜欢音乐。
She likes to listen to music.	Tā xǐhuan tīng yīnyuè.	她喜欢听音乐。
She doesn't like to listen to music.	Tā bù xǐhuan tīng yīnyuè.	她不喜欢听音乐。
He drinks coffee.	Tā hē kāfēi.	他喝咖啡。
He likes to drink coffee.	Tā xǐhuan hē kāfēi.	他喜欢喝咖啡。
He doesn't like to drink coffee.	Tā bù xǐhuan hē kāfēi.	他不喜欢喝咖啡。
They like movies.	Tāmen xǐhuan diànyǐng.	他们喜欢电影。
They like to watch movies.	Tāmen xǐhuan kàn diànyǐng.	他们喜欢看电影。
They don't like to watch movies.	Tāmen bù xǐhuan kàn diànyǐng.	他们不喜欢看电影。

At a Restaurant

At Work

Review Dialogues

Around Town

Everyday Life

Socializing

Vocabulary Builder 2

▶ 10D Vocabulary Builder 2 (CD 3, Track 20)

to stay	dāi	待 (呆)
home	jiā	家
at home	zài jiā	在家
sports	tǐyù	体育
programs	jiémù	节目
to play ball games with hands, to hit	dǎ	打
baseball	bàngqiú	棒球
basketball	lánqiú	篮球
(American) football	gǎnlǎnqiú	橄榄球
to swim	yóuyǒng	游泳
to ski	huáxuě	滑雪
Do you like ...? (lit., like or don't like?)	Xǐhuan bù xǐhuan?	喜欢不喜欢?
Do you like ...? (lit., like or don't like?)	Xǐ bù xǐhuan?	喜不喜欢?

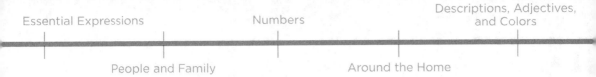
✎ Vocabulary Practice 2

Match the English word in column A with its appropriate translation in the right column.

1. *swimming*	a. zài jiā 在家
2. *Do you like … ? (lit., like or don't like?)*	b. lánqiú 篮球
3. *basketball*	c. jiémù 节目
4. *programs*	d. Xǐhuan bù xǐhuan? 喜欢不喜欢?
5. *at home*	e. yóuyǒng 游泳

ANSWER KEY
1. e; 2. d; 3. b; 4. c; 5. a

Take It Further 2

Let's focus on a few characters related to sports and other recreational activities. Notice that the character 球 qiú appears in *baseball*, *basketball*, and *football*.

体育	tǐyù	*sports*
打	dǎ	*to play ball games with hands, to hit*
棒球	bàngqiú	*baseball*
篮球	lánqiú	*basketball*
橄榄球	gǎnlǎnqiú	*American football*
游泳	yóuyǒng	*to swim*
滑雪	huáxuě	*to ski*

Let's practice those. Match the Chinese character on the left to the pīnyīn on the right, and then translate into English.

1. 篮球	a. dǎ
2. 滑雪	b. tǐyù
3. 体育	c. bàngqiú

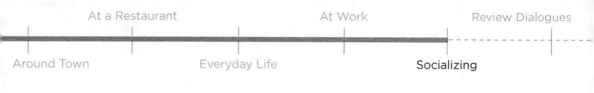

4. 橄榄球	d. huáxuě
5. 打	e. yóuyǒng
6. 游泳	f. lánqiú
7. 棒球	g. gǎnlǎnqiú

ANSWER KEY

1. f (*basketball*); 2. d (*to ski*); 3. b (*sports*); 4. g (*football*); 5. a (*to play ball games with hands, to hit*);
6. e (*to swim*); 7. c (*baseball*)

Grammar Builder 2

⏵ 10E Grammar Builder 2 (CD 3, Track 21)

To ask if someone likes something, Chinese uses a combined positive and negative: Xǐhuan bù xǐhuan? 喜欢不喜欢? (*lit., like [or] don't like*). This is often shortened to Xǐ bù xǐhuan? 喜不喜欢?

Do you like? (lit., Like [or] don't like?)	Xǐ bù xǐhuan?	喜不喜欢?
Do you like novels?	Nǐ xǐ bù xǐhuan xiǎoshuō?	你喜不喜欢小说?
I like novels.	Wǒ xǐhuan xiǎoshuō.	我喜欢小说。
Do you like to read novels?	Nǐ xǐ bù xǐhuan kàn xiǎoshuō?	你喜不喜欢看小说?
I don't like to read novels.	Wǒ bù xǐhuan kàn xiǎoshuō.	我不喜欢看小说。
Does he like to watch sports programs?	Tā xǐ bù xǐhuan kàn tǐyù jiémù?	他喜不喜欢看体育节目?
He doesn't like to watch sports programs.	Tā bù xǐhuan kàn tǐyù jiémù.	他不喜欢看体育节目。
Does she like to play basketball?	Tā xǐ bù xǐhuan dǎ lánqiú?	她喜不喜欢打篮球?
She likes to play basketball.	Tā xǐhuan dǎ lánqiú.	她喜欢打篮球。

Do they like to swim?	Tāmen xǐ bù xǐhuan yóuyǒng?	他们喜不喜欢游泳？
They don't like to swim.	Tāmen bù xǐhuan yóuyǒng.	他们不喜欢游泳。
Do you like to ski?	Nǐ xǐ bù xǐhuan huáxuě?	你喜不喜欢滑雪？
I like to ski.	Wǒ xǐhuan huáxuě.	我喜欢滑雪。

You can also use this expression to say whether or not you like someone else. (Remember that pronouns such as wǒ 我 or tā 她 can be used to mean *I* or *me*, or *she* or *her*, respectively.)

| I like her. | Wǒ xǐhuan tā. | 我喜欢她。 |
| She doesn't like me. | Tā bù xǐhuan wǒ. | 她不喜欢我。 |

✎ Work Out 1

Let's do some listening comprehension practice. Keep in mind that another way to ask questions in Chinese is to put the question particle ma 吗 at the end of the sentence. So, you could ask if someone likes something by starting with Nǐ xǐ bù xǐhuan ... 你喜不喜 ..., or with Nǐ xǐhuan ... ma? 你喜欢 ... 吗？ Now, listen to your audio, and fill in the blanks with the missing words or phrases.

▶ 10F Work Out 1 (CD 3, Track 22)

1. *Do you like to drink coffee?*

   Nǐ _____ hē kāfēi _____?

   你喜欢喝咖啡吗？

2. *You don't like to read newspapers?*

   Nǐ _____ kàn bàozhǐ ma?

   你不喜欢看报纸吗？

3. *Don't you all like to watch movies?*

Nǐmen bù xǐhuan _____ ma?

你们不喜欢看电影吗？

4. *Do you like to stay home?*

Nǐ xǐhuan dāi _____ ma?

你喜欢待在家吗？

5. *They don't like to play baseball?*

Tāmen _____ dǎ _____ ma?

他们不喜欢打棒球吗？

ANSWER KEY

1. xǐhuan, ma; **2.** bù xǐhuan; **3.** kàn diànyǐng; **4.** zài jiā; **5.** bù xǐhuan, bàngqiú

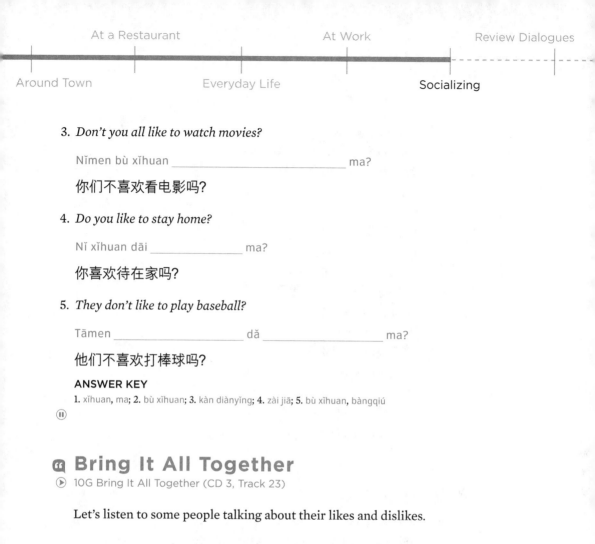

❝ Bring It All Together

▶ 10G Bring It All Together (CD 3, Track 23)

Let's listen to some people talking about their likes and dislikes.

Yáng:	Nǐ xǐhuan tīng yīnyuè ma?
	你喜欢听音乐吗？
	Do you like to listen to music?
Lán:	Wǒ bù xǐhuan.
	我不喜欢。
	I don't.
	Wǒ xǐhuan kàn diànyǐng, nǐ ne?
	我喜欢看电影，你呢？
	I like to watch movies, and you?
Yáng:	Wǒ xǐhuan kàn xiǎoshuō.
	我喜欢看小说。

I like to read novels.

Lán: Wǒ bù kàn xiǎoshuō. Wǒ kàn bàozhǐ.

我不看小说。我看报纸。

I don't read novels. I read newspapers.

Yáng: Nǐ xǐ bù xǐhuan yóuyǒng?

你喜不喜欢游泳?

Do you like swimming?

Lán: Wǒ bù xǐhuan. Wǒ xǐhuan huáxuě.

我不喜欢。我喜欢滑雪。

I don't. I like skiing.

Yáng: Nǐ dìdi xǐhuan shénme?

你弟弟喜欢什么?

What does your younger brother like?

Lán: Tā xǐhuan dāi zài jiā, kàn diànshì, shuìjiào.

他喜欢待在家，看电视，睡觉。

He likes to stay home, watch TV, [and] sleep.

⑪

✎ Work Out 2

Let's practice expressing likes and dislikes. For each question below, give both the affirmative and negative response. For example, if you see *Do you like your teacher?* You'd respond with: *I like my teacher* as well as *I don't like my teacher.*

1. *Do you like your teacher?* Nǐ xǐ bù xǐhuan nǐ lǎoshī? 你喜不喜欢你老师? _____

   _____

2. *Does your mother like to ski?* Nǐ mǔqīn xǐhuan huáxuě ma? 你母亲喜欢滑雪吗?

   _____

   _____

3. *Does his older sister like to watch movies?* Tā jiějie xǐhuan kàn diànyǐng ma? 他姐姐 喜欢看电影吗？ _____

_____

4. *Do you (pl.) like to drink tea?* Nǐmen xǐhuan hē chá ma? 你们喜欢喝茶吗？ _____

_____

5. *Does your older brother like to read novels?* Nǐ gēge xǐhuan bù xǐhuan kàn xiǎoshuō? 你哥哥喜欢不喜欢看小说？ _____

_____

6. *Does their teacher like to play baseball?* Tāmen de lǎoshī xǐ bù xǐhuan dǎ bàngqiú? 他们的老师喜不喜欢打棒球？ _____

_____

ANSWER KEY

1. Wǒ xǐhuan wǒ lǎoshī. 我喜欢我老师。 *I like my teacher.* Wǒ bù xǐhuan wǒ lǎoshī. 我不喜欢我老师。 *I don't like my teacher.* 2. Wǒ mǔqīn xǐhuan huáxuě. 我母亲喜欢滑雪。 *My mother likes to ski.* Wǒ mǔqīn bù xǐhuan huáxuě. 我母亲不喜欢滑雪。 *My mother does not like to ski.* 3. Tā jiějie xǐhuan kàn diànyǐng. 他姐姐喜欢看电影。 *His older sister likes to watch movies.* Tā jiějie bù xǐhuan kàn diànyǐng. 他姐姐不喜欢看电影。 *His older sister does not like to watch movies.* 4. Wǒmen xǐhuan hē chá. 我们喜欢喝茶。 *We like to drink tea.* Wǒmen bù xǐhuan hē chá. 我们不喜欢喝茶。 *We don't like to drink tea.* 5. Wǒ gēge xǐhuan kàn xiǎoshuō. 我哥哥喜欢看小说。 *My older brother likes to read novels.* Wǒ gēge bù xǐhuan kàn xiǎoshuō. 我哥哥不喜欢看小说。 *My older brother does not like to read novels.* 6. Tāmen de lǎoshī xǐhuan dǎ bàngqiú. 他们的老师喜欢打棒球。 *Their teacher likes to play baseball.* Tāmen de lǎoshī bù xǐhuan dǎ bàngqiú. 他们的老师不喜欢打棒球。 *Their teacher does not like to play baseball.*

▶ 10H Work Out 2 (CD 3, Track 24)

Now listen to your audio for some additional review and practice.

⏸

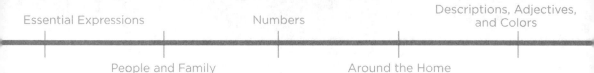
✎ Drive It Home

Let's do a little more practice expressing likes and dislikes. First, say that you like the following things: yīnyuè, tīng yīnyuè, hē kāfēi, diànyǐng, tǐyù, dāi zài jiā, bàngqiú, dǎ lánqiú (*music, listening to music, drinking coffee, movies, sports, staying at home, baseball, playing basketball*). Then, make the sentences negative to say that you don't like them.

For example, you'd start with:

Wǒ xǐhuan … (*I like …*)

Wǒ bù xǐhuan … (*I don't like …*)

Parting Words

▶ 101 Parting Words (CD 3, Track 25)

Congratulations to you. Gōngxǐ nǐ. 恭喜你。 You learned so much in this final lesson! You learned to use the negative word bù 不 to make statements and ask questions. There are many Chinese words for the word *to play*. The word dǎ 打 (*to hit*) is used for:

playing basketball	dǎ lánqiú	打篮球
playing bridge	dǎ qiáopái	打桥牌
playing drums	dǎ gǔ	打鼓

Another word tán 弹 is used for:

| *playing the piano* | tán gāngqín | 弹钢琴 |
| *playing the guitar* | tán jítā | 弹吉它 |

The general word for *playing* is wán 玩, meaning to have fun.

ⓘⓘ

And that brings us to the end of Lesson Ten of *Essential Chinese*. That means that you should know:

☐ Essential vocabulary for talking about hobbies and free time.
(Still unsure? Go back to 162.)

☐ How to express likes and dislikes.
(Still unsure? Go back to 164.)

☐ Essential vocabulary for talking about sports and recreational activities.
(Still unsure? Go back to 165.)

☐ How to ask others about their hobbies and pastimes.
(Still unsure? Go back to 167.)

☐ How to put it all together in a short conversation about free time.
(Still unsure? Go back to 169.)

Don't forget to practice and reinforce what you've learned by visiting **www.livinglanguage.com/ languagelab** for flashcards, games, and quizzes for Lesson Ten!

And that brings us to the end of our last lesson. You can test yourself and practice what you've learned with the final Word Recall, Character Recall and Quiz 2, followed by five conversational dialogues that will bring together the Chinese you've seen so far.

Word Recall

Match the English in the left column to the Chinese equivalent in the right.

1. *engineer*	a. xǐhuan 喜欢
2. *What time is it now?*	b. wǔcān 午餐
3. *time*	c. kàn 看
4. *Chinese*	d. tǐyù 体育
5. *day*	e. lǜshī 律师
6. *to watch, to read silently*	f. shíjiān 时间
7. *lunch*	g. gōngchéngshī 工程师
8. *basketball*	h. zài jiā 在家
9. *to like*	i. tiān 天
10. *to be at/go to work*	j. Xiànzài jǐ diǎn? 现在几点?
11. *week*	k. dāi 待 (呆)
12. *to listen*	l. bù 不
13. *at home*	m. kuàijìshī 会计师
14. *no, not*	n. xīngqī 星期
15. *lawyer*	o. Zhōngwén 中文
16. *sport*	p. tīng 听
17. *accountant*	q. shàng bān 上班
18. *to stay*	r. lánqiú 篮球

ANSWER KEY
1. g; 2. j; 3. f; 4. o; 5. i; 6. c; 7. b; 8. r; 9. a; 10. q; 11. n; 12. p; 13. h; 14. l; 15. e; 16. d; 17. m; 18. k

Character Recall

Let's practice some of the characters you've learned over the past several lessons. Give the pīnyīn and English for each of the following sentences. See if you can write out the sentences as well. Go slowly, stroke by stroke, and be patient with yourself. It takes practice to learn to write Chinese characters well.

1. 她喜欢听音乐。 _____

_____

2. 她不喜欢听音乐。 _____

_____

3. 他喝咖啡。 _____

_____

4. 他不喜欢喝咖啡。 _____

_____

5. 女孩看书。 _____

_____

6. 女孩喜欢看书。 _____

_____

7. 她不喜欢我。 _____

_____

8. 你喜不喜欢滑雪？ _____

_____

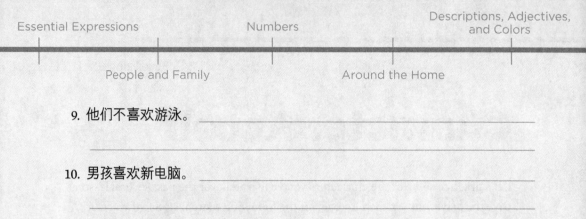

9. 他们不喜欢游泳。 _____

_____

10. 男孩喜欢新电脑。 _____

_____

ANSWER KEY

1. Tā xǐhuan tīng yīnyuè. (*She likes to listen to music.*) 2. Tā bù xǐhuan tīng yīnyuè. (*She doesn't like to listen to music.*) 3. Tā hē kāfēi. (*He drinks coffee.*) 4. Tā bù xǐhuan hē kāfēi. (*He doesn't like to drink coffee.*) 5. Nǚhái kàn shū. (*The girl reads books.*) 6. Nǚhái xǐhuan kàn shū. (*The girl likes to read books.*) 7. Tā bù xǐhuan wǒ. (*She doesn't like me.*) 8. Nǐ xǐ bù xǐhuan huáxuě? (*Do you like to ski?*) 9. Tāmen bù xǐhuan yóuyǒng. (*They don't like to swim.*) 10. Nánhái xǐhuan xīn diànnǎo. (*The boy likes the new computer.*)

Quiz 2

Xiǎokǎo 2

小考 2

Now let's review. In this section you'll find a final quiz testing what you learned in Lessons 1–10. Once you've completed it, score yourself to see how well you've done. If you find that you need to go back and review, please do so before continuing on to the final section with review dialogues and comprehension questions.

A. Match the following Chinese words to the correct English translations:

1. *what*	a. gōngzuò 工作
2. *to eat*	b. zài 在
3. *work, job, profession*	c. xǐhuan 喜欢
4. *to be (located) at*	d. shénme 什么
5. *to like*	e. chī 吃

B. Translate the following English expressions into pīnyīn:

1. *The post office is to the right of the police station.* _____

_____

2. *May I ask, do you have Peking duck?* _____

_____

3. *We eat dinner at 8:45 in the evening.* _____

_____

4. *The engineer works on Monday, Wednesday, (and) Friday.* _____

_____

5. *My mother likes to drink coffee and listen to music; my father likes to ski.* _____

_____

C. Fill in the blanks with the location word or phrase given in parentheses, and then translate your answer into English.

1. Cānguǎn zài shìchǎng _____. *(next to)*

2. Xìyuàn zài xuéxiào _____. *(south of)*

3. Lǚguǎn zài shūdiàn _____. *(to the left of)*

4. Yīyuàn zài yóujú _____. *(east of)*

5. Cèsuǒ zài _____. *(there)*

D. Fill in the blank with the most appropriate verb.

1. Tā jǐ diǎn _____ zǎocān?

2. Nǐ de dìdi_____ yīshēng ma?

3. Cānguǎn méi _____ yú.

4. Nǐmen _____ shénme yīnyuè?

5. Gēge měi tiān _____ diànshì.

E. Match the characters on the left to the pīnyīn on the right, and then give the translation.

1. 厕所	a. qù
2. 鸡	b. yīyuàn
3. 去	c. jī
4. 医院	d. hē
5. 喝	e. cèsuǒ

ANSWER KEY

A. 1. d; 2. e; 3. a; 4. b; 5. c

B. 1. Yóujú zài jǐngchá jú de yòubiān. 2. Qǐngwèn, yǒu méiyǒu Běijīng kǎo yā? 3. Wǒmen wǎnshang bā diǎn sìshíwǔ fēn chī wǎncān. 4. Gōngchéngshī xīngqī yī, xīngqī sān, xīngqī wǔ gōngzuò. 5. Wǒ de mǔqīn xǐhuan hē kāfēi, tīng yīnyuè; wǒ de fùqin xǐhuan huáxuě.

C. 1. pángbiān (*The restaurant is next to the market.*) 2. nán biān (*The theater is south of the school.*) 3. zuǒbiān (*The hotel is to the left of the bookstore.*) 4. dōng biān (*The hospital is to the east of the post office.*) 5. nàli (*The restroom is there.*)

D. 1. chī (*What time does he eat breakfast?*); 2. shì (*Is your younger brother a doctor?*) 3. yǒu (*The restaurant does not have fish.*) 4. tīng (*What kind of music do you listen to?*) 5. kàn (*[My] Older brother watches television every day.*)

E. 1. e (*restroom*); 2. c (*chicken*); 3. a (*go*); 4. b (*hospital*); 5. d (*to drink*)

How Did You Do?

Give yourself a point for every correct answer, then use the following key to determine whether or not you're ready to move on:

0–10 points: It's probably best to go back and study the lessons again to make sure you understood everything completely. Take your time; it's not a race! Make sure you spend time reviewing the vocabulary and reading through each Grammar Builder section carefully.

11–18 points: If the questions you missed were in sections A or B, you may want to review the vocabulary from previous lessons again; if you missed answers mostly in sections C or D check the Grammar Builder sections to make sure you have your grammar basics down. And if you had a hard time with section E, you should go back and review your characters!

19–25 points: Congratulations! You're doing an excellent job.

☐☐ **points**

Review Dialogues
Welcome!

Huānyíng! 欢迎! *Welcome!* Here's your chance to practice all the vocabulary and grammar you've mastered in ten lessons of *Living Language Essential Chinese* with these five everyday dialogues. Each dialogue is followed by comprehension questions.

To practice your pronunciation, don't forget to listen to the audio. As always, look for  and ⏸. You'll hear the dialogue in Chinese first, then in Chinese and English. Next, for practice, you'll do some role play by taking part in the conversation yourself!

Dialogue 1
XUÉXIÀO WǍNHUÌ
学校晚会
A PARTY AT SCHOOL

First, try to read (and listen to) the whole dialogue in Chinese. Then read and listen to the Chinese and English together. How much did you understand? Next, take part in the role play exercise in the audio and answer the comprehension questions here in the book.

Note that there will be words and phrases in these dialogues that you haven't seen yet. This is because we want to give you the feel of a real Chinese conversation. As a result, feel free to use your dictionary or the glossary if you're unclear about anything you see. And of course, you'll see the English translations for each line, as well.

▶ 12A Dialogue 1 Chinese (CD 3, Track 27), 12B Dialogue 1 Chinese and English (CD 3, Track 28), 12C Dialogue 1 Exercise (CD 3, Track 29)

Lǐ:
Duìbùqǐ.

对不起。

Excuse me.

Nǐ shì lǎoshī ma?

你是老师吗?

Are you a teacher?

Wáng:
Wǒ shì.

我是。

I am.

Lǐ:
Nǐ hǎo ma?

你好吗?

How are you?

Wáng:
Hěn hǎo. Nǐ ne?

很好。你呢?

Fine. And you?

Lǐ:
Bùcuò. Xièxie nǐ.

不错。谢谢你。

Not bad. Thank you.

Wáng:
Nǐ yǒu mèimei ma?

你有妹妹吗?

Do you have younger sisters?

Lǐ:
Wǒ yǒu gēge, yǒu dìdi. Nǐ ne?

我有哥哥,有弟弟。你呢?

I have an older brother and a younger brother. And you?

Wáng:
Wǒ yǒu jiějie, yǒu mèimei.

我有姐姐,有妹妹。

I have an older sister and a younger sister.

Lǐ:
Wǒ gēge shì lǎoshī.

我哥哥是老师。

My older brother is a teacher.

Wáng:
Tā yǒu nánxuésheng ma?

他有男学生吗?

Does he have male students?

Lǐ: Yǒu nán, yǒu nǚ.

有男，有女。

He has male and female (students). (lit., Has male, has female.)

Wáng: Wǒ jiějie shì mǔqīn.

我姐姐是母亲。

My older sister is a mother.

Tā yǒu nǚ'ér.

她有女儿。

She has a daughter.

Lǐ: Nǐ yǒu nǚ'ér ma?

你有女儿吗？

Do you have daughters?

Wáng: Wǒ yǒu érzi.

我有儿子。

I have a son.

Lǐ: Tā hǎo ma?

他好吗？

How is he?

Wáng: Hěn hǎo. Xièxie nǐ.

很好，谢谢你。

Very well. Thank you.

Lǐ: Nǐ yǒu nǚxuésheng ma?

你有女学生吗？

Do you have female students?

Wáng: Wǒ yǒu.

我有。

I do.

Nǚxuésheng shì nǐ.

女学生是你。

The female student is you.

⑪

✎ Dialogue 1 Practice

Now let's check your comprehension of the dialogue and review what you learned in Lessons 1–10. Please answer these questions in full sentences in pīnyīn. Ready?

1. Lǐ shì nǚxuésheng ma? _____

_____

2. Wáng shì lǎoshī ma? _____

_____

3. Lǐ yǒu mèimei ma? _____

_____

4. Lǐ yǒu gēge ma? _____

_____

5. Wáng yǒu méi yǒu jiějie? _____

_____

6. Lǐ de gēge zuò shénme gōngzuò? _____

_____

7. Wáng de jiějie yǒu érzi ma? _____

_____

8. Wáng yǒu méi yǒu érzi? _____

_____

ANSWER KEY

1. Lǐ shì nǚxuésheng. 2. Wáng shì lǎoshī. 3. Lǐ méi yǒu mèimei. 4. Lǐ yǒu gēge. 5. Wáng yǒu jiějie. 6. Lǐ de gēge shì lǎoshī. 7. Wáng de jiějie yǒu nǚ'ér. 8. Wáng yǒu érzi.

🔊 Dialogue 2
QÙ KĀIHUÌ
去开会
GOING TO A MEETING

As with Dialogue 1, first read and listen to the whole dialogue in Chinese. Then read and listen to the Chinese and English together. How much did you understand? Next, do the role play in the audio as well as the comprehension exercises here in the book.

▶ 13A Dialogue 2 Chinese (CD 3, Track 30), 13B Dialogue 2 Chinese and English (CD 3, Track 31), 13C Dialogue 2 Exercise (CD 3, Track 32)

Yáng:	Wǒmen yǒu jǐ gè bīngxiāng?
	我们有几个冰箱?
	How many refrigerators do we have?
Lán:	Wǒmen yǒu sì gè bīngxiāng.
	我们有四个冰箱。
	We have four refrigerators.
Yáng:	Shéi yǒu diànnǎo?
	谁有电脑?
	Who has a computer?
Lán:	Shíwǔ gè rén yǒu diànnǎo.
	十五个人有电脑。
	Fifteen people have computers.
Yáng:	Shíwǔ gè xuésheng ma?
	十五个学生吗?
	Fifteen students?
Lán:	Sì gè lǎoshī, shíyī gè xuésheng.
	四个老师，十一个学生。
	Four teachers and eleven students.
Yáng:	Zhuōzi yǐzi ne?
	桌子椅子呢?

How about tables and chairs?

Lán: Wŏmen yŏu shí zhāng zhuōzi, liùshí zhāng yĭzi.

我们有十张桌子，六十张椅子。

We have ten tables and sixty chairs.

Yáng: Wŏmen yŏu èrshíwŭ gè xuésheng, bā gè lăoshī.

我们有二十五个学生，八个老师。

We have twenty-five students and eight teachers.

Lán: Sānshísān gè rén.

三十三个人。

Thirty-three people.

Yáng: Shéi yŏu qìchē?

谁有汽车？

Who has a car?

Lán: Sān gè nǚlăoshī yŏu sì liàng qìchē.

三个女老师有四辆汽车。

Three female teachers have four cars.

Yáng: Nánlăoshī ne?

男老师呢？

And male teachers?

Lán: Yī gè nánlăoshī yŏu yī liàng.

一个男老师有一辆。

One male teacher has one.

Yáng: Wŭ gè rén yī liàng qìchē. Wŭ liàng qìchē, èrshíwŭ gè rén.

五个人一辆汽车。五辆汽车，二十五个人。

Five people per car. Five cars, twenty-five people.

Lán: Wŏ gēge yŏu yī liàng qìchē.

我哥哥有一辆汽车。

My older brother has a car.

Liù liàng qìchē, sānshí gè rén.

六辆汽车，三十个人。

Six cars, thirty people.

Yáng:	Xuésheng yǒu zìxíngchē ma?

学生有自行车吗?

Do students have bicycles?

Lán:	Xuésheng yǒu shíqī liàng zìxíngchē.

学生有十七辆自行车。

The students have seventeen bicycles.

Yáng:	Hěn hǎo.

很好。

Very good.

Ⅱ

✎ Dialogue 2 Practice

Let's practice what you've learned in this dialogue. Please answer these questions in pīnyīn.

1. Jǐ gè lǎoshī yǒu diànnǎo? _____

   _____

2. Tāmen yǒu jǐ zhāng zhuōzi? _____

   _____

3. Tāmen yǒu jiǔ gè lǎoshī ma? _____

   _____

4. Nánlǎoshī yǒu jǐ liàng qìchē? _____

   _____

5. Shéi yǒu zìxíngchē? _____

   _____

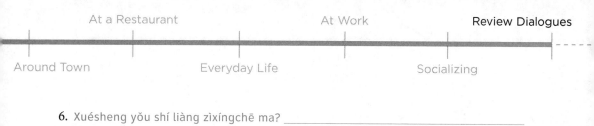
6. Xuésheng yǒu shí liàng zìxíngchē ma? _____

_____

ANSWER KEY

1. Sì gè lǎoshī yǒu diànnǎo. **2.** Tāmen yǒu shí zhāng zhuōzi. **3.** Tāmen yǒu bā gè lǎoshī. **4.** Nánlǎoshī yǒu yī liàng qìchē. **5.** Xuésheng yǒu zìxíngchē. **6.** Xuésheng you shíqī liàng zìxíngchē.

ᴖ Dialogue 3
NǏ DE JIÙ ZHÀOXIÀNGJĪ ZÀI NǍLI?
你的旧照相机在哪里？
WHERE IS YOUR OLD CAMERA?

Now let's listen to a dialogue that uses a lot of the vocabulary you learned for getting around town.

▶ 14A Dialogue 3 Chinese (CD 3, Track 33), 14B Dialogue 3 Chinese and English (CD 3, Track 34), 14C Dialogue 3 Exercise (CD 3, Track 35)

Lín:	Nǐ qù nǎli?
	你去哪里？
	Where are you going?
Zhāng:	Wǒ qù shìchǎng.
	我去市场。
	I am going to the market.
Lín:	Yóujú pángbiān de shìchǎng ma?
	邮局旁边的市场吗？
	The market next to the post office?
Zhāng:	Shì. Nǐ ne?
	是。你呢？
	Yes. And you?
Lín:	Wǒ qù xuéxiào de yīyuàn.
	我去学校的医院。
	I am going to the school's hospital.

Zhāng: Xuéxiào de yīyuàn zài nǎli?

学校的医院在哪里?

Where is the school's hospital?

Lín: Zài xuéxiào de nán biān.

在学校的南边。

On the south side of the school.

Zhāng: Wǒ mèimei shì hùshi.

我妹妹是护士。

My younger sister is a nurse.

Lín: Tā de yīyuàn zài nǎli?

她的医院在哪里?

Where is her hospital?

Zhāng: Zài xìyuàn de běi biān.

在戏院的北边。

On the north side of the theater.

Lín: Dà xìyuàn ma?

大戏院吗?

The large theater?

Zhāng: Xiǎo xìyuàn.

小戏院。

The small theater.

Zài jǐngchá jú de yòubian.

在警察局的右边。

On the right side of the police station.

Lín: Nǐ de zhàoxiàngjī shì xīn de ma?

你的照相机是新的吗?

Is your camera new?

Zhāng: Shì xīn de.

是新的。

It's new.

Lín: Nǐ de jiù zhàoxiàngjī zài nǎli?

你的旧照相机在哪里?

Where is your old camera?

Zhāng: Jiù zhàoxiàngjī zài wǒmen de cānguǎn.

旧照相机在我们的餐馆。

The old camera is at our restaurant.

Jiù zhàoxiàngjī shì wǒ mǔqīn de.

旧照相机是我母亲的。

The old camera is my mother's.

✎ Dialogue 3 Practice

Let's practice what you've learned in this dialogue. Please answer these questions in pīnyīn.

1. Shìchǎng zài nǎlǐ? _____

   _____

2. Xuéxiào de yīyuàn zài xuéxiào de xī biān ma? _____

   _____

3. Zhāng de mèimei zuò shénme gōngzuò? _____

   _____

4. Xiǎo xìyuàn de běi biān shì shénme? _____

   _____

5. Jǐngchá jú de zuǒ biān shì xiǎoxì yuàn ma? _____

   _____

6. Xīn zhàoxiàngjī zài cānguǎn ma? _____

   _____

ANSWER KEY

1. Shìchǎng zài yóujú pángbiān. 2. Xuéxiào de yīyuàn zài xuéxiào de nán biān. 3. Zhāng de mèimei shì hùshi.
4. Xiǎo xìyuàn de běi biān shì yīyuàn. 5. Jǐngchá jú de yòu biān shì xiǎo xìyuàn. 6. Jiù zhàoxiàngjī zai cānguǎn.

🔊 Dialogue 4
WǑMEN SHÉNME SHÍHOU QÙ CĀNGUǍN?
我们什么时候去餐馆?
WHEN ARE WE GOING TO THE RESTAURANT?

This time, we'll go to a Chinese restaurant. Do you remember your vocabulary related to food?

▶ 15A Dialogue 4 Chinese (CD 3, Track 36), 15B Dialogue 4 Chinese and English (CD 3, Track 37), 15C Dialogue 4 Exercise (CD 3, Track 38)

Shān:	Xiànzài jǐ diǎn? 现在几点? *What time is it?*
Jìng:	Sān diǎn sìshí fēn. 三点四十分。 *Three forty.*
Shān:	Wǎncān shì qī diǎn zhōng. Wǒmen shénme shíhou qù cānguǎn? 晚餐是七点钟。我们什么时候去餐馆? *Dinner is at seven. When do we go to the restaurant?*
Jìng:	Liù diǎn sìshíwǔ. 六点四十五。 *Six forty-five.*
Shān:	Nǐ de xuésheng ne? 你的学生呢? *How about your students?* Wǒmen gěi tāmen diǎn shénme cài? 我们给他们点什么菜? *What do we order for them?*

Jìng: Qīng zhēng yú hěn hǎo.

清蒸鱼很好。

The steamed fish is very good.

Shān: Liǎng dà wǎn páigǔ tāng.

两大碗排骨汤。

Two large bowls of spare rib soup.

Wǒmen diǎn jiǔ ma?

我们点酒吗？

Do we order wine?

Jìng: Gěi wǒmen diǎn yī píng hóngjiǔ. Gěi xuésheng diǎn píjiǔ.

给我们点一瓶红酒。给学生点啤酒。

Order one bottle of red wine for us. Beer for the students.

Shān: Kǎo niúròu ne?

烤牛肉呢？

And roast beef?

Jìng: Tāmen yǒu là niúròu ma?

他们有辣牛肉吗？

Do they have spicy beef?

Shān: Yǒu. Nǐ wǎnshang chī là de cài ma?

有。你晚上吃辣的菜吗？

They do. Do you eat spicy food in the evening?

Jìng: Wǒ chī. Wǒ zǎoshang liǎng diǎn zhōng shuìjiào.

我吃。我早上两点钟睡觉。

I do. I go to sleep at two in the morning.

✎ Dialogue 4 Practice

Let's practice what you've learned in this dialogue. Please answer these questions in pīnyīn.

1. Tāmen liù diǎn sìshíwǔ qù nǎlǐ? _____

_____

2. Shéi de xuésheng qù cānguǎn? _____

_____

3. Tāmen diǎn shénme tāng? _____

_____

4. Shéi hē píjiǔ? _____

_____

5. Jìng xǐhuan shénme niúròu? _____

_____

6. Jìng wǎnshang shí diǎn zhōng shuìjiào ma? _____

_____

ANSWER KEY

1. Tāmen liù diǎn sìshíwǔ qù cānguǎn. 2. Jìng de xuésheng qù cānguǎn. 3. Tāmen diǎn páigǔ tāng.
4. Xuésheng hē píjiǔ. 5. Jìng xǐhuan là niúròu. 6. Jìng zǎoshang liǎng diǎn zhōng shuìjiào.

🗨 Dialogue 5
NǏ XǏHUAN ZHŌNGGUÓ CÀI MA?
你喜欢中国菜吗?
DO YOU LIKE CHINESE FOOD?

Let's review some of the vocabulary and constructions you learned for talking about daily routines, and expressing likes and dislikes.

▶ 16A Dialogue 5 Chinese (CD 3, Track 39), 16B Dialogue 5 Chinese and English (CD 3, Track 40), 16C Dialogue 5 Exercise (CD 3, Track 41)

Yù: Nǐ xǐhuan kàn diànyǐng ma?

你喜欢看电影吗？

Do you like to watch movies?

Zhēn: Wǒ xǐhuan.

我喜欢。

I do.

Yù: Wǒ xīngqī sān wǎnshang qù kàn diànyǐng. Nǐ qù ma?

我星期三晚上去看电影。你去吗？

I am going to see a movie on Wednesday night. Would you go?

Zhēn: Wǒ xīngqī sān wǎnshang shàng xué.

我星期三晚上上学。

I go to school on Wednesday night.

Wǒ bā diǎn shí fēn xué Zhōngwén, jiǔ diǎn shí fēn xué diànnǎo.

我八点十分学中文，九点十分学电脑。

I study Chinese at 8:10, and computers at 9:10.

Nǐ xué shénme?

你学什么？

What do you study?

Yù: Wǒ xué kuàijì.

我学会计。

I study accounting.

Zhēn: Wǒ de mùqīn shì kuàijìshī.

我的母亲是会计师。

My mother is an accountant.

Yù: Nǐ de fùqin ne?

你的父亲呢？

And your father?

Zhēn: Tā shì lùshī.

他是律师。

He's a lawyer.

Nǐ xīngqī liù zuò shén me?

你星期六做什么？

What do you do on Saturday?

Yù: Wǒ xīngqī liù zuò shòuhuòyuán.
我星期六做售货员。
I work as a store clerk on Saturday.

Zhēn: Nǐ nǎ tiān bù gōngzuò?
你哪天不工作?
Which days don't you work?

Yù: Xīngqī sān, xīngqī wǔ, xīngqī tiān.
星期三，星期五，星期天。
Wednesday, Friday, and Sunday.

Zhēn: Nǐ xǐ bù xǐhuan xīngqī tiān qù tīng yīnyuè?
你喜不喜欢星期天去听音乐?
Do you like to listen to music on Sundays?

Yù: Wǒ xǐhuan xīngqī tiān dāi zài jiā kàn shū.
我喜欢星期天待在家看书。
I like to stay home and read on Sundays.

Zhēn: Nǐ xǐhuan hē kāfēi ma?
你喜欢喝咖啡吗?
Do you like to drink coffee?

Yù: Wǒ xǐhuan chī Zhōngguó cài.
我喜欢吃中国菜。
I like to eat Chinese food.

Zhēn: Wǒmen xiànzài qù chī.
我们现在去吃。
Let's go eat now.

Yù: Hǎo.
好。
All right.

Ⅱ

✎ Dialogue 5 Practice

Let's practice what you've learned in this dialogue. Please answer these questions in pīnyīn.

1. Shéi xǐhuan kàn diànyǐng? _____

_____

2. Yù shénme shíhou qù kàn diànyǐng? _____

_____

3. Zhēn xīngqī sān wǎnshang qù nǎli? _____

_____

4. Zhēn jiǔ diǎn shí fēn xué shénme? _____

_____

5. Yù xué fǎlǜ ma? _____

_____

6. Yù xīngqī wǔ gōngzuò ma? _____

_____

ANSWER KEY

1. Zhēn xǐhuan kàn diànyǐng. 2. Yù xīngqī sān wǎnshang qù kàn diànyǐng. 3. Zhēn xīngqī sān wǎnshang shàng xué. 4. Zhēn jiǔ diǎn shí fēn xué diànnǎo. 5. Yù xué kuàijì. 6. Yù xīngqī wǔ bù gōngzuò.

Pronunciation and Pīnyīn Guide

The Chinese language does not have an alphabet. Each word is represented by a character, which may be composed of just one stroke (line) or as many as several dozen. To represent Chinese sounds for those who do not read characters, various systems of romanization have been devised, including pīnyīn, the standard system used in China and the one most commonly used in the United States.

Each syllable in Chinese has an initial consonant sound and a final vowel sound. There are twenty-three initial sounds (consonants) and thirty-six final sounds (vowels or combinations of vowels and consonants). Here is how each sound is written in pīnyīn, with its approximate English equivalent.

INITIAL SOUNDS

PĪNYĪN	ENGLISH
b	*b* in *bear*
p	*p* in *poor*
m	*m* in *more*
f	*f* in *fake*
d	*d* in *dare*
t	*t* in *take*
n	*n* in *now*
l	*l* in *learn*
z	*ds* in *yards*
c	*ts* in *its*
s	*s* in *sing*
zh	*j* in *judge*
ch	*ch* in *church*
sh	hard *sh* in *shhhh!*
r	*r* in *rubber*
j	*dy* in *and yet*

PĪNYĪN	ENGLISH
q	*ty* in *won't you*
x	*sh* in *shoe*
g	*g* in *get*
k	*k* in *keep*
h	*h* in *help*
y	*y* in *yes*
w	*w* in *want*

FINAL SOUNDS

a	*a* in *ma*
ai	*y* in *my*
ao	*ou* in *pout*
an	*an* in *élan*
ang	*ong* in *throng*
o	*o* in *or*
ou	*oa* in *float*
ong	*ong* in *long*
e	*e* in *nerve*
ei	*ay* in *day*
en	*un* in *under*
eng	*ung* in *mung*
i (after z, c, s, zh, ch, sh)	*r* in *thunder*
i	*ee* in *see*
ia	*yah*
iao	*eow* in *meow*
ian	*yan*
iang	*yang*
ie	*ye* in *yes*

iu	*yo-yo*
iong	*young*
in	*in* in *sin*
ing	*ing* in *sing*
u	*u* in *flu*
ua	*ua* in *suave*
uai	*wi* in *wide*
uan	*wan*
uang	*wong*
uo	*wo* in *won't*
ui	*weigh*
un	*won*
ü	*like ee in see, but with lips rounded into a pout (German hübsch, French tu.)*
üan	*like ü above with an*
üe	*like ü above with e in net*
ün	*like ü above with n in an*
er	*are*

Tone Marks

Each syllable in Mandarin Chinese must be pronounced with a tone—there are four, plus a neutral tone. Here are the tone marks as they are written in pīnyīn. They're written here over the vowel *a*, which is pronounced similarly to the vowel in *John*. Imagine saying the name *John* in the following contexts:

First Tone	ā	High and neutral, no accent. Sing "John."
Second Tone	á	From middle to high, as in asking a question. "John? Is that you?"
Third Tone	ǎ	From middle to low, and then to high, as if stretching out a question: "Jo-o-o-hn, what do you think?"
Fourth Tone	à	From high to low, as if answering a question. "Who's there?" "John."

Syllables pronounced with the neutral tone are unmarked. The tones are placed over the final vowel sound of a syllable. In the case of compound vowels, such as ai, uo, ao, etc., the tone is placed over the primary vowel.

Grammar Summary

1. NUMBERS

a. Cardinal numbers 1 to 10

yī 一	one	liù 六	six
èr 二	two	qī 七	seven
sān 三	three	bā 八	eight
sì 四	four	jiŭ 九	nine
wŭ 五	five	shí 十	ten

b. Cardinal numbers 11 to 100

shíyī (10 + 1) 十一	eleven	shíliù (10 + 6) 十六	sixteen
shí'èr (10+ 2) 十二	twelve	shíqī (10 + 7) 十七	seventeen
shísān (10+ 3) 十三	thirteen	shíbā (10 + 8) 十八	eighteen
shísì (10 + 4) 十四	fourteen	shíjiŭ (10 + 9) 十九	nineteen
shíwŭ (10 + 5) 十五	fifteen	èrshí (2 x 10) 二十	twenty
sānshí (3 x 10) 三十	thirty	qīshí (7 x 10) 七十	seventy
sìshí (4 x 10) 四十	forty	bāshí (8 x 10) 八十	eighty
wŭshí (5x 10) 五十	fifty	jiŭshí (9 x 10) 九十	ninety
liùshí (6x 10) 六十	sixty	yībăi (1 x 100) 一百	one hundred

Note: The word yī 一 is added before shí 十 in numbers ending in the numerals 10 through 19.

èrshísān (20 + 3) 二十三	twenty-three	wǔshíliù (50+ 6) 五十六	fifty-six
sìshíjiǔ (40 + 9) 四十九	forty-nine	jiǔshíjiǔ (90 + 9) 九十九	ninety-nine

Note: The word yī 一 is added before shí 十 in numbers ending in the numerals 10 through 19.

c. Cardinal numbers from 200 to 100,000,000

yībǎi líng sì 一百零四	one hundred four	yīwàn 一万	ten thousand
èrbǎi/liǎngbǎi 二百	two hundred	yībǎiwàn 一百万	one million
yīqiān 一千	one thousand	yīqiānwàn 一千万	ten million
yīqiān líng sì 一千零四	one thousand four	yīyì 一亿	one hundred million
yīqiān líng sānshí'èr 一千零三十二	one thousand thirty-two	shíyì 十亿	one billion
yībǎi yīshíyī 一百一十一	one hundred eleven	sānbǎi yīshí'èr 三百一十二	three hundred twelve
èrbǎi yīshí 二百一十	two hundred ten	wǔbǎi yīshíjiǔ 五百一十九	five hundred nineteen

Note: Líng 零 is used to express the zero in numbers. Also, the number two is expressed in two different ways in Chinese. Èr 二 is used for counting and numeric expressions, such as twelve (shí'èr 十二) or two hundred (èrbǎi 二百). Liǎng 两 is used in combination with nouns.

d. Ordinal numbers (dì 第 + cardinal number)

yī 一	one	dì-yī 第一	the first
jiǔ 九	nine	dì-jiǔ 第九	the ninth

Essential Chinese

2. NOUNS

There is no distinction in form between singular and plural nouns in Chinese. To designate a plural noun use a number or a measure word in front of the noun or the ending -men for nouns referring to human beings.

yī ge píngguǒ 一个苹果	*one apple*
liǎng ge píngguǒ 两个苹果	*two apples*
Háizimen ài chī tángguǒ. 孩子们爱吃糖果。	*The children like eating candy.*

3. PERSONAL PRONOUNS

1st person (sg.)	wǒ 我	*I/me*
2nd person (sg.)	nín (fml.) 您 nǐ (infml.) 你	*you*
3rd person (sg.)	tā 他 / 她	*he, she, it/him, her, it*
1st person (pl.)	wǒmen 我们	*we/us*
2nd person (pl.)	nǐmen 你们	*you*
3rd person (pl.)	tāmen 他们	*they/them*

Note: There is no special polite form for 2nd person plural pronoun nǐmen 你们. Instead, phrases nín liǎng wèi 您两位 (*you two/both of you*) or nín jǐ wèi 您几位 (*several of you*) can be used.

4. POSSESSIVE PRONOUNS (PERSONAL PRONOUN + DE)

1st person (sg.)	wǒ de 我的	*my/mine*
2nd person (sg.)	nín de (fml.) 您的 nǐ de (infml.) 你的	*your/yours*
3rd person (sg.)	tā de 他的 / 她的	*his, her, its/his, hers, its*
1st person (pl.)	wǒmen de 我们的	*our/ours*
2nd person (pl.)	nǐmen de 你们的	*your/yours*
3rd person (pl.)	tāmen de 他们的	*their/theirs*

5. DEMONSTRATIVE PRONOUNS (ZHÈ 这 / NÀ 那 + MEASURE WORD + NOUN)

zhè běn shū 这本书	*this book*
nà běn shū 那本书	*that book*
zhèxiē shū 这些书	*these books*
nàxiē shū 那些书	*those books*

Note: Xiē 些 both makes the noun plural and serves as a measure word. Also, in colloquial language, zhè 这 and nà 那 are pronounced as zhèi 这 and nèi 那 when combined with a measure word.

6. INDEFINITE PRONOUNS

Indefinite pronouns such as anyone, anybody, anything, or anytime consist of question words + yě 也.

Rènhé 任何 (any) + yě 也 can also be used when the indefinite is a subject.

The indefinite pronouns someone and somebody are expressed with yǒu rén 有人, while the indefinite pronoun something is expressed with diǎn dōngxi 点东西.

shéi + yě (*anyone*) 谁 + 也	Wǒ shéi yě bù jiàn. 我谁也不见。	*I don't see anyone.*
shénme dōngxi + yě (*anything*) 什么东西 + 也	Tā shénme dōngxi yě chī. 他什么东西也吃。	*He eats anything.*
nǎr + yě (*anywhere*) 哪儿 + 也	Nǐ nǎr yě bù zhù. 你哪儿也不住。	*You don't live anywhere.*
shénme shíhou + yě (*anytime*) 什么时候 + 也	Nǐ xǐhuan shénme shíhou lái yě kěyǐ. 你喜欢什么时候来也可以。	*Come over anytime you like.*

shénme rén + yě (anybody) 什么人 + 也	Shénme rén yě kěyǐ qù. 什么人也可以去。	*Anybody can go.*
rènhé rén + yě (anyone) 任何人 + 也	Rènhé rén yě kěyǐ qù. 任何人也可以去。	*Anyone can go.*
rènhé dōngxi + yě (anything) 任何东西 + 也	Rènhé dōngxi yě huì biàn. 任何东西也会变。	*Anything can change.*
rènhé shíhou + yě (anytime) 任何时候 + 也	Rènhé shíhou yě kěyǐ. 任何时候也可以。	*Anytime is fine.*
rènhé dìfang + yě (anywhere) 任何地方 + 也	Rènhé dìfang yě kěyǐ. 任何地方也可以。	*Anywhere is fine. (lit., Anywhere can be.)*
yǒu rén (someone/somebody) 有人	Yǒu rén zài zhèr. 有人在这儿。	*Someone is here. (lit., There is person here.)*
méiyǒu rén (nobody) 没有人	Gōngchēzhàn méiyǒu rén. 公车站没有人。	*Nobody is at the bus stop./There are no people at the bus stop.*
diǎn dōngxi (something) 点东西	Wǒ yǒu diǎn dōngxi gěi nǐ. 我有点东西给你。	*I have something to give you.*

The indefinites shéi yě 谁也 (*anyone*) and shénme dōngxi yě 什么东西也 (*anything*) can also be translated as *everyone* and *everything*.

Shéi yě xǐhuan wǒ. 谁也喜欢我。	*Everyone loves me.*
Shénme dōngxi zuìhòu yě huì sǐ. 什么东西最后也会死。	*Everything eventually dies.*

7. MEASURE WORDS

Nouns modified by a number word or a demonstrative pronoun require a measure word (number word or demonstrative pronoun + measure word + noun). Here are some categories of measure words:

a. Nature of the object

MEASURE WORD	CATEGORY	EXAMPLES
zhī 只	*animals*	yī zhī jī 一只鸡 *(one/a chicken)* yī zhī māo 一只猫 *(one/a cat)* yī zhī niǎo 一只鸟 *(one/a bird)*
zhī 只	*utensils*	yī zhī bēi 一只杯 *(one/a cup/glass)* yī zhī wǎn 一只碗 *(one/a bowl)* yī zhī guō 一只锅 *(one/a pot)*
tái 台	*machinery*	yī tái jīqì 一台机器 *(one/a machine)* yī tái diànnǎo 一台电脑 *(one/a computer)* yī tái diànshì 一台电视 *(one/a television)*
jiàn 件	*clothing (top)*	yī jiàn chènshān 一件衬衫 *(one/a shirt)* yī jiàn fēngyī 一件风衣 *(one/a wind break)*
tiáo 条	*clothing (bottom)*	yī tiáo qúnzi 一条裙子 *(one/a skirt)*

MEASURE WORD	CATEGORY	EXAMPLES
bǎ 把	*something with handle*	yī bǎ cháhú 一把茶壶 *(one/a teapot)* yī bǎ yǔsǎn 一把雨伞 *(one/an umbrella)* yī bǎ shànzi 一把扇子 *(one/a Chinese fan)* yī bǎ yǐzi 一把椅子 *(one/a chair)*
zuò 座	*large and imposing objects*	yī zuò shān 一座山 *(one/a mountain)* yī zuò dàlóu 一座大楼 *(one/a building)*
liàng 辆	*vehicles*	yī liàng qìchē 一辆汽车 *(one/a car)*
jiā 家	*families or enterprises*	yī jiā fànguǎn 一家饭馆 *(one/a restaurant)* liǎng jiā rénjia 两家人家 *(two families)*
ge 个	*people*	yī ge rén 一个人 *(one/a person)* liǎng ge lǎoshī 两个老师 *(two teachers)*

b. Shape of the object

MEASURE WORD	CATEGORY	EXAMPLES
zhāng 张	*flat surface*	yī zhāng zhǐ 一张纸 (*one/a piece of paper*) yī zhāng bàozhǐ 一张报纸 (*one/a newspaper*) yī zhāng zhàopiàn 一张照片 (*one/a photo*) yī zhāng chuáng 一张床 (*one/a bed*)
zhī 支	*pointed and thin or like a branch*	yī zhī bǐ 一支笔 (*one/a pen*) yī zhī qiāng 一支枪 (*one/a gun*) yī zhī jūnduì 一支军队 (*one/a troop*)
lì 粒	*granular*	yī lì mǐ 一粒米 (*one/a grain of rice*) yī lì zhǒngzi 一粒种子 (*one/a seed*)
kē 颗	*small and round*	yī kē yǎnlèi 一颗眼泪 (*one/a tear drop*) yī kē hóngdòu 一颗红豆 (*one/a red bean*)
tiáo 条	*long and thin*	yī tiáo lù 一条路 (*one/a road*) yī tiáo sījīn 一条丝巾 (*one/a silk scarf*) yī tiáo xiàn 一条线 (*one/a string*)

MEASURE WORD	CATEGORY	EXAMPLES
pán 盘	*something round and flat or shaped like a plate*	yī pán wéiqí 一盘围棋 *(one/a game of Chinese checkers)* yī pán cídài 一盘磁带 *(one/a tape)*

c. Containers that function as measure words

MEASURE WORD	CATEGORY	EXAMPLES
bēi 杯	*cup*	yī bēi shuǐ 一杯水 *(one/a cup of water)*
dài 袋	*bag*	yī dài píngguǒ 一袋苹果 *(one/a bag of apples)*
pán 盘	*plate*	yī pán cài 一盘菜 *(one/a dish)*
xiāng 箱	*box*	yī xiāng lājī 一箱垃圾 *(one/a box of rubbish)*

d. Measure words denoting quantity

MEASURE WORD	CATEGORY	EXAMPLES
duì 对	*pair*	yī duì ěrhuán 一对耳环 *(a pair of earrings)*
shuāng 双	*pair*	yī shuāng wàzi 一双袜子 *(one/a pair of socks)* yī shuāng yǎnjing 一双眼睛 *(one/a pair of eyes)*
fù 副	*pair*	yī fù yǎnjìng 一副眼镜 *(one/a pair of glasses)*

MEASURE WORD	CATEGORY	EXAMPLES
qún 群	*group*	yī qún yāzi 一群鸭子 *(one/a group of ducks)* yī qún rén 一群人 *(one/a group of people)*
dá 打	*dozen*	yī dá jīdàn 一打鸡蛋 *(one/a dozen eggs)*
chuàn 串	*cluster*	yī chuàn pútáo 一串葡萄 *(one/a cluster of grapes)*

f. Amounts or portions of things

MEASURE WORD	CATEGORY	EXAMPLES
kuài 块	*piece*	yī kuài dàngāo 一块蛋糕 *(one/a piece of cake)*
dī 滴	*drop*	yī dī shuǐ 一滴水 *(one/a drop of water)*
cè 册	*volume*	yī cè shū 一册书 *(one/a volume of a set of books)*

j. Units of measurement

cùn 寸	*inch*	chǐ 尺	*foot*
yīnglǐ 英里	*mile*	gōngchǐ/mǐ 公尺／米	*meter*
gōnglǐ 公里	*kilometer*	gōngjīn 公斤	*kilogram*
jīn 斤	*catty*	bàng 磅	*pound*

The table below shows the different units of measure used in mainland China, Taiwan and Hong Kong.

UNITS OF MEASURE	MAINLAND CHINA	TAIWAN	HONG KONG
Length	mǐ 米 *(meter)/* gōnglǐ 公里 *(kilometer)*	mǐ 米 *(meter)/* gōnglǐ 公里 *(kilometer)*	chǐ 尺 *(foot)/* gōnglǐ 公里 *(kilometer)*
Weight	gōngjīn 公斤 *(kilogram)*	gōngjīn 公斤 *(kilogram)*	bàng 磅*(pound)/* gōngjīn 公斤 *(kilogram)/* jīn 斤 *(catty)*

k. The measure word gè 个

Used especially with those nouns that don't have particular measure words assigned or abstract things

yī ge píngguǒ 一个苹果	*one/an apple*
yī ge zhàoxiàngjī 一个照相机	*one/a camera*
yī ge xīngqī 一个星期	*one/a week*
yī ge mèng 一个梦	*one/a dream*
yī ge zhǔyi 一个主意	*one/an idea*

l. More than one measure word may be possible.

yī tái diànnǎo 一台电脑 *or* yī bù diànnǎo 一部电脑	*one/a computer*
yī ge diànyǐng 一个电影 *or* yī bù diànyǐng 一部电影	*one/a film*

8. VERB-OBJECT VERBS VS. TWO-SYLLABLE VERBS

"Verb-object" verbs, such as chīfàn 吃饭 (*lit., to eat cooked rice*), consist of a verb plus an implicit (often not translated) object in that order. They differ from ordinary two syllable verbs such as míngbái 明白 (*to understand*) and rènshi 认识 (*to know someone*) in that:

Only "verb-object" verbs can be split by a particle, such as le 了.

In adverbial constructions that follow the pattern verb + object + duplicated verb + de 得, only the verb of "verb-object" verbs is repeated.

Wǒ chīfàn. 我吃饭。	*I eat.*
Wǒ chīle fàn. 我吃了饭。	*I ate.*
Wǒ jiǎnchá le. 我检查了。	*I examined (someone or something).*
Wǒ (de) māma zuòfàn zuò de hěn hǎo. 我(的)妈妈做饭做得很好。	*My mother cooks very well.*

9. EXPRESSING *TO BE*

Use hěn 很 (*very*) not shì 是 to connect nouns and adjectives.

Tā hěn gāo. 他很高。	*He is tall. (lit., he very tall)*

Use shì 是 between a subject noun and a predicate noun in an equational sentence.

Měiguó de shǒudū shì Huáshèngdùn. 美国的首都是华盛顿。	*America's capital is Washington.*
Jīngyú shì yī zhǒng dòngwù. 鲸鱼是一种动物。	*The whale is one kind of animal.*

Shì 是 is used to indicate existence or a state of being (see 19 below).

10. VERB PARTICLES

In Chinese, time expressions often fulfill the role that tense endings and auxiliaries do in English.

Míngtiān wǒ chūchāi.	明天我出差。	*Tomorrow I'm going on a business trip.*

Verbal particles are used to encode information related to verbs such as completion, duration, and future intent.

a. Completed actions: Le 了

Le 了 indicates something is different from the way it was in the past and can be used to refer to things that have not yet happened.

Tā qùle Shànghǎi. 他去上海。	*He went to Shanghai.*
Qiūtiān láile. 秋天来了。	*Now it's autumn.*
Fēijī kuài qǐfēi le. 飞机快起飞了。	*The plane is about to take off.*

b. Actions that took place from a time in the past to now: Guò 过

Wǒ qù guò Zhōngguó. 我去过中国。	*I have been to China.*
Nǐ qù guò Zhōngguó méiyǒu? 你去过中国没有?	*Have you ever been to China?*
Wǒ qù guò. 我去过。	*Yes, I have been.*
Wǒ hái méi qùguò. 我还没去过。	*No, I haven't been yet.*
Wǒ méi(yǒu) qùguò. 我没（有）去过。	*No, I have never been before.*

c. Continuous actions and states: Zài 在 and Zhe 着

Zài 在 refers to a continuous activity.

Wǒ zài kànshū. 我在看书。	*I am reading.*
Tāmen zài gōngzuò. 他们在工作。	*They are working.*
Tā zài chuān yīfu. 她在穿衣服。	*She is putting on clothes.*

Zhe 着 refers to a state of events that continues in time.

Tā zhànzhe. 他站着。	*He is standing.*
Nǐ názhe yī běn shū. 你拿着一本 书。	*You are holding a book.*
Tā chuānzhe yī jiàn hóngsè de yīfu. 她穿着一件红色的衣服。	*She is wearing a red piece of clothing.*

d. Future actions: Huì 会

One use of huì is to express that an action will (possibly) take place in the future.

Wǒ míngtiān huì qù Shànghǎi.	我明天会去上海。	*I'll (probably) go to Shanghai tomorrow.*

11. NEGATION

Bù 不 is used with the present, future or continuous tense and zài.

Méiyǒu 没有 is used with completed actions (translated into present perfect in English).

Wǒ bù xǐhuan yú. 我不喜欢鱼。	*I don't like fish.*
Wǒ de māma hái méiyǒu chīfàn. 我的妈妈还没有吃饭。	*My mother hasn't eaten yet.*

12. COMMANDS

Commands are formed by simply using a verb without any subject. You can soften the tone of a command by using the particle ba 吧 after the verb. To make a negative command add bié 别 (or bùyào 不要) in front of the verb.

Shuì! 睡!	*Sleep!*
Shuì ba. 睡吧。	*Go to sleep.*
Bié shuì. 别睡。	*Don't sleep.*

13. ADVERBIAL USE OF DE 得

verb + de 得 + adjective

Tā chī de hěn kuài. 他吃得很快。	*He eats very fast.*
Nǐ shuō de hěn hǎo. 你说得很好。	*You speak very well.*

verb + object + verb + de 得 + adjective

Wǒ shuō Zhōngwén shuō de hěn bù hǎo. 我说中文说得很不好。	*I don't speak Chinese very well. (lit., I speak Chinese not very well.)*

Note that, in Chinese characters, de 得 differs from the possessive de 的, although both have the same pronunciation.

14. QUANTIFIERS (*MANY, SOME, ALL, EVERY*)

hěn duō 很多 (*many*)	Zhōngguó yǒu hěn duō ré. 中国有很多人。	*There are a lot of people in China.*
bù shǎo 不少 (*many*)	Wǒ yǒu bù shǎo gǒu. 我有不少狗。	*I have quite a few dogs.*
yīxiē 一些 (*some*)	Tā yǒu yīxiē wèntí. 他有一些问题。	*He has some questions.*
quánbù 全部 (*all*)	Quánbù rén dōu zǒu le. 全部人都走了。	*All the people are gone.*
měi 每 (*every*) + *measure word*	Měi ge rén dōu zǒu le. 每个人都走了。	*Everyone is gone.*

All and *every* can formed by duplicating a measure word and using dōu 都 before the main verb. Used with subjects that denote two things or people, dōu 都 means both.

Měi ge rén dōu xǐhuan tā. 每个人都喜欢他。	*Everyone likes him. (lit., All the people like him.)*

Běnběn shū dōu hěn guì. 本本书都很贵。	Every book is expensive./All books are expensive.
Huáng xiānsheng hé Huáng tàitai dōu bù zài. 黄先生和黄太太都不在。	Both Mr. Huang and Mrs. Huang are not here.
Bob, Bill hé Susie dōu shì xuésheng. 鲍勃，比尔和苏西是学生。	Bob, Bill, and Susie are all students.
Wǒmen dōu shì Měiguórén. 我们都是美国人。	We are all American.

15. COMPARISON

a. Comparative adjectives: A bǐ 比 B + adjective + (exact degree of difference)

Wǒ bǐ nǐ dà. 我比你大。	I am older than you. (lit., I am bigger than you.)
Zhè běn shū bǐ nà běn shū guì. 这本书比那本书贵。	This book is more expensive than that one.
Wǒ bǐ nǐ dà sān suì. 我比你大三岁。	I am three years older than you.

b. Comparative adverbs: A + verb + de bǐ 的比 + B + adverb

| Wǒ zǒu de bǐ nǐ kuài.
我走得比你快。 | I walk faster than you do. |

c. Expressing similarity: yǒu … nàme 有...那么 (as … as) or A + hé 和 + B + yīyàng 一样 + adjective

| Wǒ yǒu nǐ nàme gāo. 我有你那么高。 | I am as tall as you. |
| Wǒ hé nǐ yīyàng gāo. 我和你一样高。 | I am as tall as you. (lit., I and you are the same height.) |

d. Superlative: zuì 最 + adjective

Zhè jiā lǚdiàn zuì hǎo. 这家旅店最好。	*This hotel is the best.*
Tā de chē zuì kuài. 他的车最快。	*His car is the fastest.*

16. YES/NO QUESTIONS

a. The question particle ma 吗 (declarative sentence + ma 吗)

Nǐ qù ma? 你去吗?	*Do you go?*
Wǒ qù. 我去。	*Yes, I do.*
Zhāng xiānsheng zhù zài zhèr ma? 张先生住在这儿吗?	*Does Mr. Zhang live here?*
Tā zhù zài zhèr. 他住在这儿。	*Yes, he does.*
Tā pǎo de kuài ma? 他跑得快吗?	*Does he run fast?*
Tā pǎo de kuài. 他跑得快。	*Yes, he does.*

b. verb/adverb + bù 不 + verb/adverb

Nǐ qù bù qù? 你去不去?	*Do you go or not?*
Wǒ qù. 我去。	*Yes, I do.*
Tā pǎo de kuài bù kuài? 他跑得快不快?	*Does he run fast?*
Tā pǎo de kuài. 他跑得快。	*Yes, he does.*

c. ne 呢 (*how about … ?*)

Nǐ xǐhuan hē chá ma? 你喜欢喝茶吗?	*Do you like drinking tea?*
Wǒ xǐhuan. Nǐ ne? 我喜欢，你呢?	*Yes, I do. How about you?*

d. Answering yes/no questions

Repeat the (auxliary) verb in positive or negative form.

Nǐ shì Zhāng xiǎojie ma? 你是张小姐吗?	*Are you Miss Zhang?*
Wǒ shì. 我是。	*Yes, I am.*
Wǒ bù shì. 我不是。	*No, I am not.*
Nǐ huì shuō Yīngwén ma? 你会说英文吗?	*Do you know how to speak English?*
Wǒ huì. 我会。	*Yes, I do.*
Wǒ bù huì. 我不会。	*No, I don't.*

e. Answering negative questions

Opposite of English pattern

Nǐ méiyǒu qián ma? 你没有钱吗?	*Don't you have money?*
Bù shì. Wǒ yǒu. 不是。我有。	*Yes. I have (money). (lit., No. I have money.)*
Shì. Wǒ méiyǒu. 是。我没有。	*No. I don't (have money). (lit., Yes. I don't have money.)*

17. QUESTION WORDS

shénme 什么	*what*
shénme shíhou 什么时候	*when*
nǎli/nǎr 哪里 / 那儿	*where*
nǎ/něi + *measure word* 哪	*which (sg.)*
nǎ/něi + xiē 哪 + 些	*which (pl.)*
shéi 谁	*who/whom*
duōshǎo qián 多少钱	*how much (money)*
duōshǎo/jǐ + *measure word* 多少 / 几	*how many*
duōshǎo 多少	*how much*

zěnme (yàng) 怎么（样）	*how*
wèishénme 为什么	*why*

Note: Question words do not move to the front of the sentence as they do in English. The order is that of so-called "echo questions," e.g. Tā shì shéi? 他／她是谁？ *Who is he/she? (lit., He/she is who?)*.

18. USE OF THE PREPOSITION ZÀI 在 AND OTHER LOCATION WORDS

The preposition zài 在 (*at, in, on*) is used to specify location. No form of *to be* is necessary in Chinese.

Wǒ zài xuéxiào (lǐ). 我在学校（里）。	*I am in school.*
Tā zài Měiguó. 他在美国。	*He is in the U.S.*

qiánbiān 前边	*in front of*
hòubiān 后边	*behind*
shàngbiān 上边	*above*
xiàbiān 下边	*under*
zuǒbiān 左边	*the left*
yòubiān 右边	*the right*
pángbiān 旁边	*beside*
zhōngjiān 中间	*between*
lǐ(biān) 里（边）	*inside/in*
wàibiān 外边	*outside*

zài 在 + location word + place or object name

Wǒ de shū zài zhuōzi de xiàbiān. 我的书在桌子的下边。	*My book is under the table.*

Note: The positioning of zhōngjiān 中间 is different: "A hé B de zhōngjiān A 和 B 的 中间," where A and B are separate place names or words.

19. *THERE IS/ARE*: YǑU 有 AND SHÌ 是

place word + location word + yǒu 有 + subject

Xuéxiào (lǐ) yǒu hěnduō xuésheng. 学校（里）有很多学生。	There are a lot of students in the school. (lit., School inside there are lots of students.)
Gōngyuán lǐ yǒu yī tiáo gǒu. 公园里有一条狗。	There is a dog in the park. (lit., Park inside there is a dog.)

place word + location word + shì 是 + place word

Gōngyuán de hòubiān shì xuéxiào. 公园的后边是学校。	There is a school behind the park. (lit., The back of the park is school.)

Note: Shì 是 can only be used to assert the existence of singular nouns.

20. HERE IS A LIST OF THE ONE HUNDRED MOST ESSENTIAL CHINESE CHARACTERS:

CHARACTER	PRONUNCIATION	MEANING
一	yī	*one*
二	èr	*two*
三	sān	*three*
四	sì	*four*
五	wǔ	*five*
六	liù	*six*
七	qī	*seven*
八	bā	*eight*
九	jiǔ	*nine*
十	shí	*ten*
百	bǎi	*hundred*
千	qiān	*thousand*
万	wàn	*ten thousand*
大	dà	*big*
中	zhōng	*middle*
小	xiǎo	*small*
车	chē	*car*
电	diàn	*electricity*
云	yún	*cloud*
雨	yǔ	*rain*
火	huǒ	*fire*
水	shuǐ	*water*
山	shān	*mountain*
上	shàng	*on, above*
下	xià	*under*
左	zuǒ	*left*

CHARACTER	PRONUNCIATION	MEANING
右	yòu	*right*
前	qián	*in front of*
后	hòu	*behind*
书	shū	*book*
菜	cài	*dish, vegetable*
鸡	jī	*chicken*
鸭	yā	*duck*
牛	niú	*cow*
羊	yáng	*sheep*
猪	zhū	*pig*
鱼	yú	*fish*
酒	jiǔ	*wine*
笔	bǐ	*pen*
字	zì	*character*
是	shì	*to be*
几	jǐ	*several*
美	měi	*beautiful*
国	guó	*country*
高	gāo	*tall, high*
低	dī	*low*
不	bù	*not*
没	méi	*not to have*
有	yǒu	*to have, there is/there are*
也	yě	*also*
了	le	*(verb suffix)*
东	dōng	*east*
南	nán	*south*
西	xī	*west*

CHARACTER	PRONUNCIATION	MEANING
北	běi	*north*
人	rén	*people*
今	jīn	*at present*
我	wǒ	*I, me*
你	nǐ	*you*
他	tā	*he*
她	tā	*she*
来	lái	*come*
去	qù	*go*
们	men	*(plural particle)*
做	zuò	*do*
元	yuán	*dollar*
两	liǎng	*two*
再	zài	*again*
见	jiàn	*see*
刀	dāo	*knife*
分	fēn	*separate, minute, cent*
到	dào	*until, reach*
力	lì	*strength*
加	jiā	*plus*
又	yòu	*also*
口	kǒu	*mouth*
门	mén	*door*
叫	jiào	*call*
名	míng	*first name*
和	hé	*and*
茶	chá	*tea*
在	zài	*in, on, at*

CHARACTER	PRONUNCIATION	MEANING
坐	zuò	*sit*
报	bào	*report, newspaper*
外	wài	*outside*
内	nèi	*inside*
天	tiān	*sky*
太	tài	*too (excessive), very*
好	hǎo	*good, well*
姓	xìng	*last name*
学	xué	*learn*
文	wén	*written language*
家	jiā	*home, family*
写	xiě	*write*
对	duì	*correct*
老	lǎo	*old*
年	nián	*year*
月	yuè	*month, moon*
日	rì	*day, sun*
从	cóng	*from*

21. IMPORTANT SIGNS IN CHINESE CHARACTERS:

CHARACTER	MEANING
男	*Men*
女	*Women*
卫生间 *or* 厕所 *or* 洗手间	*Lavatory, Toilet, Restroom*
有人	*Occupied (lit., there is person)*
无人	*Vacant (lit., there is no person)*
不准抽烟	*No Smoking*
不准进入	*No Admittance*

CHARACTER	MEANING
敲	*Knock*
铃	*Ring, Bell*
私人	*Private*
查询	*Inquire Within*
停! / 止步!	*Stop!*
去!	*Go!*
小心!	*Look out!*
危险!	*Danger!*
慢走	*Go slowly!*
绕道	*Detour*
警告	*Caution*
保持右走	*Keep to the Right*
桥	*Bridge*
不准停车	*No Parking*
衣帽间	*Check Room*
兑换	*Money Exchange*
资料	*Information*
等候室	*Waiting Room*
不要伸出窗外	*Don't Lean Out (of the Window)*
飞机场	*Airport*
铁路	*Railroad*
快车	*Express (lit., fast car)*
慢车	*Local (lit., slow car)*
站	*Stop (bus, train, etc.)*
不可张贴	*Post No Bills*
修理中	*Under Repair*
入口	*Entrance*
出口	*Exit*

CHARACTER	MEANING
配家具房子	*Furnished Rooms*
房子	*House*
油漆未干	*Wet Paint*
十字路口	*Crossroads*
肉店	*Butcher*
饼店	*Bakery*
牛奶	*Milk*
裁缝店	*Tailor Shop*
鞋店	*Shoe Store*
理发店	*Barber Shop*
菜市场 / 市场	*Grocer, Market*
药房 / 药店	*Pharmacy, Drugstore*
糖果店	*Confectioner, Candy Store*
文具店	*Stationery Store*
信箱	*Mail Box*
酒吧	*Bar, Tavern*
公安局	*Police Station*
酒	*Wines*
油站	*Gas Station*
书店	*Book Store*
市政府	*City Hall*
点心 / 小吃	*Refreshments, Snacks*
(冷) 水	*(Cold) Water*
(热) 水	*(Hot) Water*

Glossary

English - Chinese

A

a few/a little yī diǎndiǎn 一点点
a little more of … zài lái yìdiǎn … 再来一点 …
a long time hěn jiǔ 很久
a lot hěn duō 很多
a while yī huìr 一会儿
abdominal pain (to have) dùzi tòng 肚子痛
able (to be) kěyǐ 可以 (in terms of permission),
  néng(gòu) 能(够) (in terms of proficiency)
about dàgài 大概, dàyuē 大约
academic performance chéngjì 成绩
accounting kuàijì 会计
  accountant kuàijìshī 会计师
across the street duìmiàn 对面
address dìzhǐ 地址
adjectival particle de 的
adverbial particle de 得
after zhīhòu 之后
after that ránhòu 然后
afternoon xiàwǔ 下午
afterwards ránhòu 然后
again zài 再
ago yǐqián 以前
airport jīchǎng 机场
  airplane fēijī 飞机, fēijī chǎng 飞机场
alcoholic drink jiǔ 酒
all dōu 都
all gone guāng 光
allow (to) ràng 让
  allowed (to be) kěyǐ 可以
almost chàbùduō 差不多
  almost time to do something (lit. quickly …
    as of now) Kuài … le. 快 … 了。
alright hǎo ba 好吧
also yě 也, háiyǒu 还有
always zǒngshì 总是
America Měiguó 美国
  American (people) Měiguórén 美国人
and hé 和
and (for connecting two adjectives or
  adverbs) yòu … yòu … 又 … 又 …
another zài lái … 再来 …
anyone shénme rén yě, shéi yě 什么人也, 谁也
anything shénme dōngxi yě 什么东西也
anywhere nǎr, nǎli yě 哪儿, 哪里也

apartment gōngyù 公寓
appear to be kàn qǐlái 看起来
apple píngguǒ 苹果
apply (to) shēnqǐng 申请
approximately dàgài 大概
April sì yuè 四月
around zuǒyòu 左右
as … adjective/adverb as … (used for people and
  things nearby) yǒu … zhème 有 … 这么
  as … adjective/adverb as … (used for people and
    things far away) yǒu … nàme 有 … 那么
ask (to) wèn 问
  ask directions (to) (lit., to ask the road) wènlù
    问路
at zài 在
attend (a) class (to) shàngkè 上课
attend university (to) shàng dàxué 上大学
audit a class (to) pángtīng 旁听
August bā yuè 八月
aunt
  aunt (father's older brother's wife) bómǔ 伯母
  aunt (father's sister) gūgu 姑姑
  aunt (father's younger brother's wife) shěnshen
    婶婶
  aunt (mother's brother's wife) jiùmǔ/jiùmā
    舅母/舅妈
  aunt (mother's sister) yímǔ/yímā 姨母/姨妈
Australia Àozhōu 澳洲
  Australian Àozhōurén 澳洲人
autumn qiūtiān 秋天

B

back (body) bèibù 背部
bad huài 坏
badminton yǔmáoqiú 羽毛球
bag bāo 包
ball qiú 球
banana xiāngjiāo 香蕉
bandage to a wound (to) bāozā shāngkǒu
  包扎伤口
baseball bàngqiú 棒球
basketball lánqiú 篮球
bathroom wèishēngjiān 卫生间
be (to) shì 是
  be (located) at (to) zài 在
beautiful piàoliang 漂亮
because yīnwèi 因为
bed chuáng 床

bedroom wòfáng 卧房
beef niúròu 牛肉
beer píjiǔ 啤酒
before zhīqián 之前
behind hòubiān 后边
belly dùzi 肚子
belt pídài 皮带
between zhōngjiān 中间
  between … and … zài … hé … zhōngjiān
  在 … 和 … 中间
bicycle zìxíngchē 自行车
big dà 大
biology shēngwù 生物
birthday shēngrì 生日
bitter kǔ 苦
black hēi 黑
  black pepper hēi hújiāo 黑胡椒
bleed (to) liúxiě 流血
block lùkǒu 路口
blow (to) chuī 吹
blue lán 蓝
book shū 书
  bookstore shūdiàn 书店
  bookshelf shūjià 书架
boots xuēzi 靴子
boss lǎobǎn 老板
bottle píng 瓶
box hé 盒
boy nánháir 男孩儿, nánhái 男孩
bowl wǎn 碗
bread miànbāo 面包
breakfast zǎocān 早餐
bridge qiáo 桥
bring (to) gěi 给
  bring me … Gěi wǒ … 给我
Britain Yīngguó 英国
  British (people) Yīngguórén 英国人
brother (older) gēge 哥哥
  brother (younger) dìdi 弟弟
brown zōngsè 棕色
building dàlóu 大楼
bunch (as in cluster) chuàn 串
bus gōngchē 公车
  bus stop gōngchē zhàn 公车站
butter huángyóu 黄油
buy (to) mǎi 买

C

cabbage bāoxīncài 包心菜
cafeteria shítáng 食堂
cake dàngāo 蛋糕
calf xiǎotuǐ 小腿
call (to) jiào 叫
  called (to be) (full name) jiào 叫
  called (to be) (surname) xìng 姓
campus xiàoyuán 校园
can (noun) guàn 罐
Canada Jiānádà 加拿大
Cantonese Guǎngdōngrén 广东人
car chē, qìchē 车, 汽车
careful (to be) xiǎoxīn 小心
carp lǐyú 鲤鱼
carrot húluóbo 胡萝卜
carton hé 盒
cash xiànjīn 现金
cat māo 猫
  catch a cold (to) zháoliáng 着凉
CD jīguāng chàngpiàn 激光唱片
celery qíncài 芹菜
cereal màipiàn 麦片
chair yǐzi 椅子
change (monetary) língqián 零钱
change trains/subways/buses (to) huàn chē
换车
check (payment) zhīpiào 支票
  Check please! Qǐng nǐ jiézhàng! 请你结帐!
check (to) jiǎnchá 检查
  check (someone's) pulse (to) bǎmài 把脉
cheek liǎnjiá 脸颊
chemistry huàxué 化学
chest xiōngbù 胸部
  chest pain (to have) xiōngbù tòng 胸部痛
chicken jī 鸡
  chicken meat (boneless) jīròu 鸡肉
China Zhōngguó 中国
  Chinese (language) Zhōngwén 中文
  Chinese (people) Zhōngguórén 中国人
  Chinese cuisine Zhōngcài 中菜
chocolate qiǎokèlì 巧克力
chopsticks kuàizi 筷子
church jiàotáng 教堂
cinema diànyǐngyuàn 电影院
city chéngshì 城市
class kè 课

classmate tóngxué 同学

classroom jiàoshì 教室

classical music gǔdiǎn yīnyuè 古典音乐

clean gānjìng 干净

clean (to) qīnglǐ 清理

clock shízhōng 时钟

close (to) guān 关

clothes, clothing yīfu 衣服

clothing store fúzhuāng diàn 服装店

coat wàitào 外套

coffee kāfēi 咖啡

cold lěng 冷

cold (sickness) gǎnmào 感冒

colleague tóngshì 同事

color sè 色, yánsè 颜色

come (to) lái 来

come over (to) guòlái 过来

come in jìnlái 进来

company gōngsī 公司

comparatively bǐjiào 比较

computer diànnǎo 电脑

concentrate (to) jízhōng jīngshén 集中精神

Congratulations! Gōngxǐ nǐ! 恭喜你!

cook (to) shāocài 烧菜, shāofàn 烧饭,
zuòfàn 做饭

cooked rice fàn 饭

cooking pēngrèn 烹饪

corner lùkǒu 路口

cost of living shēnghuófèi 生活费

cough késou 咳嗽

Could you ... ? (lit., bother you) máfan nǐ
麻烦你

Could I trouble you for ... Máfan nǐ gěi wǒmen
... 麻烦你给我们 ...

cousin

cousin (father's brother's daughter, older than
you) tángjiě 堂姐

cousin (father's brother's daughter, younger
than you) tángmèi 堂妹

cousin (father's brother's son, older than
you) tánggē 堂哥

cousin (father's brother's son, younger than
you) tángdì 堂弟

cross the street (to) guò mǎlù 过马路

crowded yōngjǐ 拥挤

cucumber huángguā 黄瓜

culottes qúnkù 裙裤

cup bēizi 杯子

currency unit, equivalent to the dollar
unit yuán 元

colloquial word for yuán kuài 块

one one-hundredth of a yuán, equivalent to the
cent fēn 分

one tenth of a yuán, equivalent to the dime jiǎo 角

colloquial word for jiǎo máo 毛

cycling qí zìxíngchē 骑自行车

D

dance (to) tiàowǔ 跳舞

dark shēn 深

daughter nǚ'ér 女儿

day tiān 天

deadline zuìhòu qīxiàn 最后期限

December shí'èr yuè 十二月

degree (temperature) dù 度

delicious hǎochī 好吃

department (college level) xì 系

department store bǎihuò gōngsī 百货公司

dessert tiándiǎn 甜点

diarrhea (to have) lā dùzi 拉肚子

dictionary zìdiǎn 字典

different bùtóng 不同

difficult nán 难

dim sum diǎnxīn 点心

dining room fàntīng 饭厅

dinner wǎncān 晚餐

dirty zāng 脏

discount (to give a) dǎzhé 打折

discuss (to) tántan 谈谈

dish of food cài 菜

dislike (to) bù xǐhuan 不喜欢

do (to) zuò 做

doctor yīshēng 医生

document wénjiàn 文件

dog gǒu 狗

Don't worry. Méi shì. 没事。

dormitory sùshè 宿舍

dress liányīqún 连衣裙

drink (to) hē 喝

drive (a car) (to) kāichē 开车

duck yā 鸭

E

each měi 每

ear ěrduo 耳朵

east dōng 东

eat (to) chī 吃
economize (to) shěng 省
egg(s) jīdàn 鸡蛋
eight bā 八
either ... or ... huòzhě 或者
elbow zhǒu 肘
electronics store (lit., home appliances
  store) jiāyòng diànqì diàn 家用电器店
elephant xiàng 象
eleven shíyī 十一
employee gùyuán 雇员
engineering gōngchéng 工程
  engineer gōngchéngshī 工程师
English (language) Yīngwén 英文
enlightened kāimíng 开明
even more gèng 更
evening wǎn 晚, wǎnshang 晚上
every měi 每
  every day měi tiān 每天
  everyone měi ge rén 每个人
  everything yīqiè 一切
examination kǎoshì 考试
examine (to) jiǎnchá 检查
exchange (to) huàn 换
Excuse me. Láojià. 劳驾。
Excuse me. (apologizing) Duìbùqǐ. 对不起。
  (asking for a favor), guì 贵expensive
extracurricular activities kèwài huódòng
  课外活动
eye yǎnjing 眼睛

F _____

face liǎn 脸
familiar with (to be) shúxī 熟悉
family jiā 家
far yuǎn 远
fashionable shímáo 时髦
fast kuài 快
father fùqin 父亲
  dad bàba 爸爸
fax machine chuánzhēnjī 传真机
fear (to) pà 怕
February èr yuè 二月
feel (to) gǎndào 感到
  feel dizzy (to) tóuyūn 头晕
  feel nauseous (to) ěxin 恶心
  feel unwell(to) bù shūfu 不舒服
female nǚ 女

fever (to have a) fāshāo 发烧
fewer than (lit. not enough) bù gòu 不够
file dǎng'àn 档案, wénjiàn 文件
  filing cabinet dǎng'àn guì 档案柜
film diànyǐng 电影
finally zhōngyú 终于
find (to) zhǎo 找
fine hǎo 好
finger shǒuzhǐ 手指
  fingernail zhǐjia 指甲
finish class (to) fàngxué 放学
first xiān 先
fish yú 鱼
  fishing diàoyú 钓鱼
five wǔ 五
food fàn 饭, shíwù 食物
  food market càishìchǎng 菜市场
foot jiǎo 脚
football (American) gǎnlǎnqiú 橄榄球
for example bǐrú 比如
forehead étóu 额头
foreign wàiguó 外国
  foreign language wàiyǔ 外语
forget (to) wàng 忘
fork chāzi 叉子
forty sìshí 四十
four sì 四
France Fǎguó 法国
  French (people) Fǎguórén 法国人
  French (language) Fǎwén 法文
frequently jīngcháng 经常
Friday xīngqī wǔ 星期五
friend péngyou 朋友
from cóng 从
  from ... to ... cóng ... dào ... 从 ... 到 ...
fruit shuǐguǒ 水果

G _____

garlic suàntóu 蒜头
Germany Déguó 德国
  German (people) Déguórén 德国人
  German (language) Déwén 德文
get off (to) (a vehicle) xià chē 下车
get on (to) (a vehicle) shàng chē 上车
get out chùqù 出去
girl nǚháir 女孩儿, nǚhái 女孩, nǚháizi 女孩子
give (to) gěi 给
  Give me another ... Zài gěi wǒ ... 再给我 ...

Give me … Gěi wǒ … 给我

give/get an injection (to) dǎ zhēn 打针

glass bēizi 杯子

glass (measure word) bēi 杯

go (to) qù 去

go to the hospital (to) qù yīyuàn 去医院

go abroad (to) chūguó 出国

Go ahead. Hǎo ba. 好吧。

go ahead (to) wǎng qián 往前, zǒu ba 走吧

go online (to) shàngwǎng 上网

go straight ahead (to) yīzhí wǎng qián zǒu
一直往前走

go to a clinic (to) qù zhěnsuǒ 去诊所

go to a movie/the movies (to) kàn diànyǐng
看电影

go to a stadium (to) qù tǐyùguǎn 去体育馆

go to class (to), to start class shàngkè 上课

go to school (to), to attend school shàngxué
上学

go to the beach (to) qù hǎitān 去海滩

go to work (to), be at work (to) shàngbān 上班

gold jīnsè 金色

good hǎo 好

goodbye zàijiàn. 再见。

graduate (to) bìyè 毕业

graduate student yánjiūshēng 研究生

graduate school yánjiūyuàn, yánjiūsuǒ 研究院,
研究所

grandfather

grandfather (maternal side) wàigōng 外公

grandfather (paternal side) yéye 爷爷

grandmother

grandmother (maternal side) wàipó 外婆

grandmother (paternal side) nǎinai 奶奶

grape pútao 葡萄

grasp (to) bǎ 把

green lǜ 绿, lǜsè 绿色

grey huīsè 灰色

H

half bàn 半

ham huǒtuǐ 火腿

hand shǒu 手

happy kuàilè 快乐

hat màozi 帽子

have (to) yǒu 有

Do (you) have … ? … yǒu méiyǒu … ?
… 有没有 … ?

Do you have … ? Nǐmen yǒu … ma?
你们有 … 吗?

don't/doesn't have méiyǒu 没有

have a chat (to) tántan 谈谈

Have a seat. Qǐng zuò. 请坐。

have fun (to) wán de kāixīn 玩得开心

have to (to) bìxū 必须

he tā 他

headache (to have a) tóu tòng 头痛

hear (to) tīngdào 听到

heel zúgēn 足跟

hello Nǐ hǎo. 你好。

help (to) bāngzhù 帮助

her (object pronoun) tā 她

her (possessive pronoun) tā de 她的

here zhèlǐ 这里

hers tā de 她的

hiking yuǎnzú 远足

him tā 他

his tā de 他的

history lìshǐ 历史

hit (to) dǎ 打

hobbies àihào 爱好

hockey qūgùnqiú 曲棍球

hold (to) ná 拿

holiday jiàqī 假期

home jiā 家

homework gōngkè 功课

Hongkongese Xiānggǎngrén 香港人

hospital yīyuàn 医院

hot là 辣, tàng 烫

hotel lǚguǎn 旅馆, lǚdiàn 旅店, jiǔdiàn 酒店

hour (amount of time) xiǎoshí 小时, zhōngtóu 钟头

hour (o'clock) diǎn, diǎn zhōng 点, 点钟

house fángzi 房子

how zěnme yang? 怎么样, zěnyàng 怎样

how far? yǒu duō yuǎn? 有多远?

how long? duōjiǔ 多久

how many? jǐ 几?

How much?/ How many? duōshǎo 多少

how to get to … ? zěnme zǒu 怎么走

hungry è 饿

husband xiānsheng 先生

I

I wǒ 我

I don't want to … Wǒ bù xiǎng … 我不想 …

I need … Wǒ yào … 我要 …

I would like to have ... Wǒ xiǎng yào ... 我想
要 ...

I'm sorry Duìbùqǐ. 对不起。

I'm sorry. (lit., to find it embarrassing (to do
something)) Bù hǎoyìsi. 不好意思。

ice cream bīngjílíng 冰激凌

if rúguǒ 如果

  if ... (then) rǔguǒ ... jiù 如果 ... 就

illness bìng 病

in lǐ 里, zài 在

  in a hurry, in a rush cōngmáng 匆忙

  in addition háiyǒu 还有

  in front of qiánbiān 前边, ménkǒu 门口

  in style shímáo 时髦

  in this/that case ... nà ... 那 ...

inexpensive piányi 便宜

inflammation fāyán 发炎

inside lǐbiān 里边

instant noodles fāngbiànmiàn 方便面

intelligent cōngmíng 聪明

interest xìngqù 兴趣

intersection lùkǒu 路口, shízì lùkǒu 十字路口

interview miànshì 面试

It's nothing. (Don't worry. No problem.)
  Méi shì. 没事。

it's only ... zhǐshì 只是

Italy Yìdàlì 意大利

  Italian (people) Yìdàlìrén 意大利人

  Italian (language) Yìdàlìwén意大利文

its tā de 它的

J

jacket jiákè 夹克

January yī yuè 一月

Japan Rìběn 日本

  Japanese (people) Rìběnrén 日本人

  Japanese (language) Rìwén 日文

job gōngzuò 工作

jogging huǎnbùpǎo 缓步跑, mànpǎo 慢跑

jot something down (to) jì xiàlái 记下来

juice guǒzhī 果汁

July qī yuè 七月

June liù yuè 六月

just now gāngcái 刚才

K

keep (to) liú 留

kick (to) tī 踢

kilogram gōngjīn 公斤

kilometers gōnglǐ 公里

kind (noun) zhǒng 种

kitchen chúfáng 厨房

knife dāo 刀

knitting biānzhī 编织

know a fact (to), know something (to)
  zhīdào 知道

  know (to) (someone) rènshi 认识

  know how to (to) huì 会

L

laboratory shíyànshì 实验室

laborer gōngrén 工人

large dà 大

large (size) dàhào 大号

last month shàng ge yuè 上个月

last week shàng ge lǐbài 上个礼拜

last year qùnián 去年

late night snack yèxiāo 夜宵, xiāoyè 宵夜

law fǎlǜ 法律

lawyer lǜshī 律师

learn (to) xué 学

leave zǒu 走

  Leave. (polite) Zǒu ba. 走吧。

  leave a message (to) liúyán 留言

  leave one's own country (to) chūguó 出国

left zuǒ 左

left side (of) (the) zuǒbiān 左边

leg tuǐ 腿

less and less or more and more yuè lái yuè
越来越

let (to) ràng 让

  let me ràng wǒ 让我

  let ... ràng ... ba 让 ... 吧

library túshūguǎn 图书馆

  library card túshūzhèng 图书证

lie down (to) tǎng 躺

light qiǎn 浅

  light green qiǎn lǜsè 浅绿色

like (to) xǐhuan 喜欢

lips zuǐchún 嘴唇

listen (to) tīng 听

live in (to) zhù zài 住在

lively, busy, bustling rènào 热闹

living room kètīng 客厅

lobster lóngxiā 龙虾

look (to) kàn 看

look for (to) zhǎo 找
love (to) ài 爱
lunch wǔcān 午餐

M

Mahjong Májiàng 麻将
major zhuānyè, zhǔxiū 专业, 主修
make (to) zuò 做
  make a date (to) yuē 约
  make a medical house call (a doctor) (to) chū zhěn 出诊
  make a phone call (to) dǎ diànhuà 打电话
  make an appointment (to) yuē 约, yùyuē 预约
male nán 男
man nánrén 男人
many, much hěn duō 很多
  many times hěn duō cì 很多次
March sān yuè 三月
market shìchǎng 市场
May wǔ yuè 五月
May I … qǐng nǐ/nín 请你/您
  May I ask … ? qǐng wèn 请问
  May I have… ? (lit., Could you give me… ?)
    Nǐ kěyǐ gěi wǒ … ma? 你可以给我 … 吗?
maybe kěnéng 可能
me wǒ 我
meal fàn 饭
measure word for books, photo albums, magazines běn 本
measure word for cars, taxis, bicycles liǎng 两
measure word for plants kē 棵
measure word for bottled drinks píng 瓶
measure word for automobiles, bicycles, carts liàng 辆
measure word for garments worn over the lower half of the body, or for objects that are long and thin (scarves), also for animals (dogs, fish, bulls…) tiáo 条
measure word for garments worn over the upper part or full length of the body jiàn 件
measure word for knives bǎ 把
measure word for machines tái 台
measure word for meal dùn 顿
measure word for number of family members kǒu 口
measure word for objects that are pointed and thin, utensils, and some animals zhī 只
measure word for objects that are small and

round chuàn 串
measure word for objects that have a flat surface (tables, desks, chairs …) zhāng 张
measure word for people, cities, groups, and nations gè 个
measure word for small plants and vegetables kē 颗
measure word for soup, rice (bowl) wǎn 碗
measure word for tables, desks, chairs zhāng 张
measure word for tile, tablets, other thin and flat objects piàn 片
measure word for water, coffee, tea, wine (cup, glass) bēi 杯
measure word of general unit for ordering food (dish, plate) pán 盘
meat ròu 肉
(medication) taken after a meal fàn hòu fú 饭后服
(medication) taken before a meal fàn qián fú 饭前服
medium (size) zhōnghào 中号
meet (to) rènshi 认识
meeting huìyì 会议
  have a meeting (to) kāihuì 开会
  in a meeting (to be) kāihuì 开会
menu càidān 菜单
meters mǐ 米
midnight bànyè 半夜
milk niúnǎi 牛奶
  milk tea nǎichá 奶茶
mine wǒ de 我的
minute fēn 分
  minute(s) fēnzhōng 分钟, fēn 分
Miss xiǎojie 小姐
Monday xīngqī yī 星期一
money qián 钱
more and more yuè lái yuè 越来越
moreover érqiě 而且
morning zǎoshang 早上
mother mǔqīn 母亲
  mom māma 妈妈
motorcycle mótuōchē 摩托车
mouth zuǐba 嘴巴, kǒu 口
movie diànyǐng 电影
  movie theater diànyǐngyuàn 电影院
Mr. xiānsheng 先生
Mrs. tàitai 太太

museum bówùguǎn 博物馆
mushrooms mógu 蘑菇
music yīnyuè 音乐
must bìxū 必须
mustard jièmò 芥末
my wǒ de 我的

N

Nanjingese Nánjīngrén 南京人
napa cabbage báicài 白菜
napkin cānjīn 餐巾
near jìn 近
  nearby fùjìn 附近
neck bózi 脖子
neighbor línjū 邻居
never cónglái méiyǒu... 从来没有...
new xīn 新
newspaper bàozhǐ 报纸
next week xià ge lǐbài 下个礼拜
next month xià ge yuè 下个月
next year míngnián 明年
next to pángbiān 旁边
night wǎnshang 晚上
nine jiǔ 九
nineteen shíjiǔ 十九
Ninety jiǔshí 九十
no, not bù 不
  negative particle used for commands bié 别,
    bùyào 不要
  no need to bùyòng 不用
  No problem. Méi shì. 没事。Méiyǒu wèntí.
    没有问题。
  Not bad. Bùcuò. 不错
noisy chǎo 吵
noodles miàntiáo 面条
noon zhōngwǔ 中午
north běi 北
nose bízi 鼻子
novel xiǎoshuō 小说
November shíyī yuè 十一月
now xiànzài 现在
nurse hùshi 护士

O

o'clock diǎn, diǎn zhōng 点, 点钟
October shí yuè 十月
of course dāngrán 当然
office bàngōngshì 办公室

official Chinese currency Rénmínbì 人民币
often jīngcháng 经常
ok hǎo ba 好吧
  ... is it alright? ... hǎo bù hǎo? ... 好不好?
old (things) jiù 旧
on zài 在
  on (top of) shàngbiān 上边, shàng, 上
  on foot zǒulù 走路
  on the corner zài lùkǒu 在路口
  on/to the left zài zuǒbiān 在左边
  on the phone jiǎng diànhuà 讲电话
  on/to the right zài yòubiān 在右边
  on time zhǔnshí 准时
  on vacation fàngjià 放假
one yī 一
  one dozen yī dǎ 一打
  one hundred yībǎi 一百
  one million yībǎiwàn 一百万
  one more zài lái ... 再来...
  one thousand yīqiān 一千
onion yángcōng 洋葱
open (to) chǎngkāi 敞开
  open (the mouth) (to) zhāngkāi 张开
  open-minded kāimíng 开明
or (suggesting a preference) háishì 还是
orange (color) júsè 橘色
orange (fruit) júzi 橘子
order (to) (food) diǎn 点
  order a dish (to) diǎn cài 点菜
ought to yīnggāi 应该
our wǒmen de 我们的
ours wǒmen de 我们的
out of style guòshí 过时
outside wàibiān 外边
over there zài nàli 在那里

P

painting túhuà 图画
pair shuāng 双
pants kùzi 裤子
paper zhǐ 纸
parent jiāzhǎng 家长
park gōngyuán 公园
particle for softening commands ba 吧
particle indicating completion of an
  action guò 过
particle indicating an ongoing action zài 在
particle indicating an ongoing state of

being zhe 着
particle indicating that an action has been completed le 了
particle used for comparison (than) bǐ 比
part-time job jiānzhí 兼职
pay (to) fù 付
  pay by check (to) yòng zhīpiào fùqián 用支票付钱
  pay by credit card (to) shuākǎ 刷卡
  pay in cash (to) fù xiànjīn 付现金
Peking duck Běijīng (kǎo) yā 北京烤鸭
Pekingese Běijīngrén 北京人
pen bǐ 笔
pepper hújiāo 胡椒
perhaps kěnéng 可能
person, people rén 人
pharmacy yàofáng 药房
philosophy zhéxué 哲学
photograph zhàopiàn 照片
physics wùlǐ 物理
pink fěnhóngsè 粉红色
place lǐ 里
  placed first (to be) pái dì yī míng 排第一名
plan (to) dǎsuan 打算
plaster cast (to have a) dǎ shígāo 打石膏
plate pánzi 盘子
play (ball games with hands, bridge or drums) (to) dǎ 打
  play (piano) (to), to pluck tán 弹
  play a game (to) wán yóuxì 玩游戏
  play a sport (to) zuò yùndòng 做运动
  play ball (to) dǎ qiú 打球
  play drums (to) dǎ gǔ 打鼓
  play piano (to) tán gāngqín 弹钢琴
  play soccer (to) tī zúqiú 踢足球
  play the flute (to) chuī dízi 吹笛子
  play violin (to) lā xiǎotíqín 拉小提琴
please (used to make an invitation or ask a favor) qǐng 请
  Please say that again. Qǐng zài shuō yī cì. 请再说一次。
  Please sit. Qǐng zuò. 请坐。
  please ... (lit., please you ...) qǐng nǐ/nín 请你/您
poetry shī 诗
police officer jǐngchá 警察
  police station jǐngchá jú 警察局
polite kèqi 客气

popular liúxíng 流行
  pop music liúxíng yīnyuè 流行音乐
pork zhūròu 猪肉
  pork chop(s) zhūpái 猪排
  twice-cooked pork huíguōròu 回锅肉
possessive particle de 的
post office yóujú 邮局
potatoe(s) mǎlíngshǔ 马铃薯, tǔdòu 土豆
pound bàng 磅
practice (to) liànxí 练习
prefix for ordinal numbers dì 第
prepare (to) zhǔnbèi 准备
  prepare for a lesson (to) yùxí 预习
pretty piàoliang 漂亮
pretty good bùcuò 不错
principal xiàozhǎng 校长
printer dǎyìnjī 打印机, yìnbiǎojī 印表机
private tutoring sīrén bǔxí 私人补习
profession gōngzuò 工作
program, show jiémù 节目
pull (to) lā 拉
purple zǐsè 紫色
put (to) fàng 放

Q

quarter of an hour kè 刻
question particle ma 吗
quick kuài 快
quite tǐng 挺

R

radio shōuyīnjī 收音机
rainbow cǎihóng 彩虹
raincoat yǔyī 雨衣
read (to) kàn 看
  read a map (to) kàn dìtú 看地图
  read a book kàn shū 看书
red hóng 红, hóngsè 红色
  red wine hóngjiǔ 红酒
reference book cānkǎoshū 参考书
refrigerator bīngxiāng 冰箱
relatively bǐjiào 比较
remind (to) tíxǐng 提醒
rest (to) xiūxi 休息
restaurant cānguǎn 餐馆, fànguǎn 饭馆
restroom cèsuǒ 厕所, xǐshǒujiān 洗手间
review (to) wēnxí 温习
  review a lesson (to) fùxí 复习

ride (to) qí 骑

right yòu 右

  right side (of) (the) yòubiān 右边

ring jièzhi 戒指

road lù 路

roast kǎo 烤

  roast chicken kǎo jī 烤鸡

room fángjiān 房间

rose méiguì 玫瑰

Russian (language) Éwén 俄文

S

salad shālā 沙拉

salary xīnshuǐ 薪水

salty xián 咸

same yīyàng 一样

Saturday xīngqī liù 星期六

save (to) (as in to store up) chǔ 储, cún 存

say (to) shuō 说

scalding tàng 烫

scared of (to be) pà 怕

school xuéxiào 学校

season jìjié 季节

second(s) miǎo 秒

see (to) kànjiàn 看见, jiàn 见, kàn 看

  see a play (to) kàn xìjù 看戏剧

See you later! Děng huìr jiàn! 等会见!

  See you next time! Xià cì jiàn! 下次见!

  See you soon! Huítóu jiàn! 回头见!

self zìjǐ 自己

send a fax (to) fā chuánzhēn 发传真

September jiǔ yuè 九月

seven qī 七

several jǐ ge 几个

  several days jǐ tiān 几天

  several times jǐ cì 几次

Shanghaiese Shànghǎirén 上海人

she tā 她

ship chuán 船

shirt chènshān 衬衫

sister

  sister (older) jiějie 姐姐

  sister (younger) mèimei 妹妹

sore throat (to have a) sǎngzi tòng 嗓子痛

stomachache (to have a) wèi tòng 胃痛

shiver (to) fādǒu 发抖

shoes xiézi 鞋子

  shoestore xiédiàn 鞋店

shop shāngdiàn 商店

should yīnggāi 应该

shoulder jiānbǎng 肩膀

shrimp xiā 虾

shut (to) guān 关

sibling xiōngdìjiěmèi 兄弟姐妹

sick (to be) bìngle 病了

sidewalk rénxíngdào 人行道

silver yínsè 银色

sing (to) chànggē 唱歌

sit (to) zuò 坐

six liù 六

ski (to) huáxuě 滑雪

skirt qúnzi 裙子

skort qúnkù 裙裤

sleep (to) shuì 睡

  sleep (to) shuìjiào 睡, 睡觉

slice (measure word) piàn 片

slow, slowly màn 慢

small xiǎo 小, xiǎohào 小号

  small town xiǎo zhèn 小镇

sneakers yùndòngxié 运动鞋

soccer (football) zúqiú 足球

socks wàzi 袜子

soda sūdǎ shuǐ 苏打水

sofa shāfā 沙发

some yīxiē 一些

  someone yǒu rén 有人

  something (yī)diǎn dōngxi, (yī)xiē dōngxi
    (一) 点东西, (一) 些东西

  something to drink hē de 喝的

son érzi 儿子

soup tāng 汤

sour suān 酸

south nán 南

soy sauce jiàngyóu 酱油

Spain Xībānyá 西班牙

  Spanish (people) Xībānyárén 西班牙人

  Spanish (language) Xībānyáwén 西班牙文

spare ribs páigǔ 排骨

speak (to) shuō 说

spicy là 辣

spoon tāngchí 汤匙, sháozi 勺子

sport tǐyù 体育

spring chūntiān 春天

  spring rolls chūnjuǎn 春卷

staff yuángōng 员工, gōngzuò rényuán 工作人员

stand (to) zhàn 站

start (to) kāishǐ 开始
stay (to) dāi 待 (呆), liú 留
steak niúpái 牛排
steamed qīng zhēng 清蒸
  steamed fish qīng zhēng yú 清蒸鱼
still haí 还
stir-fried chǎo 炒
stir-fried dish chǎocài 炒菜
stitch up (to) (a wound) féngxiàn 缝线
store shāngdiàn 商店
  store clerk shòuhuòyuán 售货员
straight yīzhí 一直
street jiē 街
string beans sìjìdòu 四季豆
strong qiángzhuàng 强壮
student xuésheng 学生
study (to) xué 学
style kuǎnshì 款式
submit homework (to) jiāo gōngkè 交功课
subway dìtiě 地铁
  subway station dìtiě zhàn 地铁站
such as bǐrú 比如
sugar táng 糖
summer xiàtiān 夏天
Sunday xīngqī tiān 星期天
supper wǎncān 晚餐
supplement (to) (money) bāngbǔ 帮补
surname xìng 姓
sweater máoyī 毛衣
sweet tián 甜
swim (to) yóuyǒng 游泳

T

table zhuōzi 桌子
Taiji / Tai Chi Tàijíquán 太极拳
take (to) ná 拿
  take (to) (a form of transportation) zuò 坐, dā 搭
  take a business trip (to) chūchāi 出差
  take a cardiogram (to) zuò xīndiàntú 做心电图
  take medicine (to) chī yào 吃药
  take personal leave (to) qǐng (shì)jià 请事假
  take sick leave (to) qǐng bìngjià 请病假
  take (someone's) temperature (to) liáng tǐwēn 量体温
tall gāo 高
taste (to) cháng 尝
taxi chūzūchē 出租车
tea chá 茶

teach (to) jiāo 教
teacher lǎoshī 老师
telephone diànhuà 电话
  telephone booth diànhuàtíng 电话亭
television diànshì 电视
temperature (body) tǐwēn 体温
ten shí 十
ten thousand yīwàn 一万
tender nèn 嫩
tennis wǎngqiú 网球
test (to) kǎo 考
  test, to take an exam kǎoshì 考试
textbook kèběn 课本
Thank you. Xièxie. 谢谢。
that nà 那
the best zuì hǎo de 最好的
the most zuì 最
the year after next hòunián 后年
the year before last qiánnián 前年
theater xìyuàn 戏院
their/theirs tāmen de 他们的
them tāmen 他们
then ránhòu 然后
there nàli 那里
there is/there are yǒu 有
therefore suǒyǐ 所以
these zhèxiē 这些
they tāmen 他们
thigh dàtuǐ 大腿
think (to) xiǎng 想
thirteen shísān 十三
thirty sānshí 三十
this zhè 这
  this afternoon jīntiān xiàwǔ 今天下午
  this month zhège yuè 这个月
  this morning jīntiān zǎoshang 今天早上
  this way zhèbiān 这边
  this week zhège lǐbài 这个礼拜
  this year jīnnián 今年
those nàxiē 那些
three sān 三
throat sǎngzi 嗓子
Thursday xīng qī sì 星期四
ticket piào 票
tidy (to) qīnglǐ 清理
tie the score (to) dǎ chéng píngshǒu 打成平手
tight jǐn 紧
time (in broad terms) shíhou 时候

time (in hours and minutes) shíjiān 时间
time off fàngjià 放假
time(s) biàn 遍, cì 次
to, before (ten minutes to/before one
o'clock) chà (chà shí fēn yī diǎn), 差
(差十分一点)
today jīntiān 今天
together yīqǐ 一起
tomato fānqié 番茄
tomorrow míngtiān 明天
the day after tomorrow hòutiān 后天
tongue shétou 舌头
tonight jīntiān wǎnshang 今天晚上
too tài 太
tooth yáchǐ 牙齿
traditional Chinese dress qípáo 旗袍
traffic light hónglǜdēng 红绿灯
train station huǒchēzhàn 火车站
travel lǚxíng 旅行
trendy liúxíng 流行
trouble (to) máfan 麻烦
trunk bízi 鼻子
T-shirt T-xùshān/hànshān T-恤衫/汗衫
Tuesday xīngqī èr 星期二
turn
turn around the corner guǎi ge wān 拐个弯
turn left wǎng zuǒ zhuǎn 往左转
turn right wǎng yòu zhuǎn 往右转
twelve shí'èr 十二
twenty èrshí 二十
two èr 二
two (used to describe amount) liǎng 两

U

uncle
uncle (father's older brother) bóbo 伯伯
uncle (father's sister's husband) gūfu 姑夫
uncle (father's younger brother) shūshu 叔叔
uncle (mother's brother) jiùjiu 舅舅
uncle (mother's sister's husband) yífu 姨夫
under xiàbiān, xià 下边, 下
underpants nèikù 内裤
underpass rénxíng dìdào 人行地道
understand (to) míngbái 明白
university dàxué 大学
us wǒmen 我们
usually tōngcháng 通常

V

vacation jiàqī 假期
vanilla xiāngcǎo 香草
vegetables shūcài 蔬菜
vegetarian chīsù 吃素
very fēicháng 非常, tǐng挺, hěn很
volleyball páiqiú 排球
vomit (to) tùle 吐了

W

wait (to) děng 等
walk (to) zǒu 走
want (to) yào 要
Do you want … ? Nǐ yào…ma? 你要 … 吗?
want (to), would like … xiǎng 想
wash (to) xǐ 洗
watch shǒubiǎo 手表
watch (to) kàn 看
watch TV (to) kàn diànshì 看电视
water shuǐ 水
we wǒmen 我们
wear (to) chuān 穿
Wednesday xīngqī sān 星期三
week xīngqī 星期
week lǐbài 礼拜
weekday (lit., workday) gōngzuòrì 工作日
weekend zhōumò 周末
well hǎo 好
well … nà 那
west xī 西
western cuisine xī càn 西餐
what shénme 什么
What nationality? Nǎ guórén? 哪国人?
what time shénme shíhou 什么时候
What time is it now? Xiànzài jǐdiǎn? 现在几点?
what time? jǐdiǎn 几点
what's more … érqiě 而且
when jǐdiǎn 几点, shénme shíhou 什么时候
where nǎli 哪里
Where (at)? Where is … ? zài nǎli? 在哪里?
which nǎ 哪
which day nǎ tiān 哪天
which place nǎli 哪里
which station nǎge zhàn 哪个站
white bái, báisè 白, 白色
who, whom shéi 谁
whole body quánshēn 全身

why wèishénme 为什么
wife tàitai 太太
will huì 会
wine hóngjiǔ 红酒, jiǔ 酒
winter dōngtiān 冬天
woman nǚrén 女人
work gōngzuò 工作
  work overtime (to) jiābān 加班
  worker gōngrén 工人
wrist shǒuwàn 手腕
writing xiězuò 写作

Y

year nián 年
yellow huáng 黄, huángsè 黄色
yesterday zuótiān 昨天
  the day before yesterday qiántiān 前天
yoga yújiā 瑜伽
you nǐ 你
you (plural) nǐmen 你们
You're welcome. Bù kèqi. 不客气。
young lady xiǎojie 小姐
young, youthful niánqīng 年轻
your (plural) nǐmen de 你们的
your (singular) nǐ de 你的
your (fml.) nín de (fml.) 您的 (fml.)
yours (fml., plural) nǐmen de 你们的

Z

zero líng 零

Chinese - English

A

ài 爱 to love
àihào 爱好 hobbies
Àozhōu 澳洲 Australia
Àozhōurén 澳洲人 Australian

B

bā yuè 八月 August
bā 八 eight
ba 吧 particle for softening commands
bǎ 把 to grasp, measure word for knives
bàba 爸爸 dad
bái 白 white
báicài 白菜 napa cabbage
bǎihuò gōngsī 百货公司 department store
báisè 白色 white
bǎmài 把脉 to check (someone's) pulse
bàngōngshì 办公室 office
bàn 半 half
bàngqiú 棒球 baseball
bàng 磅 pound
bāngbǔ 帮补 to supplement (money)
bāngzhù 帮助 to help
bànyè 半夜 midnight
bāo 包 bag
bāoxīncài 包心菜 cabbage
bāozā shāngkǒu 包扎伤口 to bandage to a wound
bàozhǐ 报纸 newspaper
bēi 杯 measure word for water, coffee, tea, wine; cup, glass
běi 北 north
bèibù 背部 back
Běijīng (kǎo) yā 北京烤鸭 Peking duck
Běijīngrén 北京人 Pekingese
bēizi 杯子 cup, glass
běn 本 measure word for books, photo albums, magazines
bǐ 比 particle used for comparison (than)
bǐ 笔 pen
biàn 遍 times
biānzhī 编织 knitting
biǎodì 表弟 cousin (mother's sibling's or father's sister's son, younger than you)
biǎogē 表哥 cousin (mother's sibling's or father's

sister's son, older than you)

biǎojiě 表姐 cousin (mother's sibling's or father's sister's daughter, older than you)

biǎomèi 表妹 cousin (mother's sibling's or father's sister's daughter, younger than you)

bié 别 negative particle used for commands

bǐjiào 比较 relatively, comparatively

bìng 病 illness

bīngjílíng 冰激凌 ice cream

bìngle 病了 be sick

bīngxiāng 冰箱 refrigerator

bǐrú 比如 such as, for example

bìxū 必须 to have to, must

bìyè 毕业 to graduate

bízi 鼻子 nose, trunk

bóbo 伯伯 uncle (father's older brother)

bómǔ 伯母 aunt (father's older brother's wife)

bówùguǎn 博物馆 museum

bózi 脖子 neck

bù 不 no, not

bùcuò 不错 pretty good, not bad

bù gòu 不够 fewer than (lit. not enough)

Bù hǎoyìsi. 不好意思。 I'm sorry. (lit., to find it embarrassing (to do something))

Bù kèqi. 不客气。 You're welcome.

bù shūfu 不舒服 to feel unwell

bù xǐhuan 不喜欢 to dislike

bùtóng 不同 different

bùyào 不要 negative particle used for commands

bùyòng 不用 no need to

C

cài 菜 dish of food

càidān 菜单 menu

cǎihóng 彩虹 rainbow

càishìchǎng 菜市场 food market

cānguǎn 餐馆 restaurant

cānjīn 餐巾 napkin

cānkǎoshū 参考书 reference book

cèsuǒ 厕所 restroom

chá 茶 tea

chà (chà shí fēn yī diǎn) 差 (差十分一点) to, before (ten minutes to/before one o'clock)

chàbùduō 差不多 almost

cháng 尝 to taste

chǎng 敞 to open

chànggē 唱歌 to sing

chǎo 吵 noisy

chǎo 炒 stir-fried

chǎocài 炒菜 stir-fried dish

chāzi 叉子 fork

chē 车 car

chéngjì 成绩 academic performance

chéngshì 城市 city

chènshān 衬衫 shirt

chī yào 吃药 to take medicine

chī 吃 to eat

chīsù 吃素 vegetarian

chū zhěn 出诊 to make a medical house call (a doctor)

chǔ 储 to save

chuàn 串 measure word for objects that are small and round, bunch, cluster

chuān 穿 to wear

chuán 船 ship

chuáng 床 bed

chuánzhēnjī 传真机 fax machine

chūchāi 出差 to take a business trip

chúfáng 厨房 kitchen

chūguó 出国 to leave one's own country, to go abroad

chuī dízi 吹笛子 to play the flute

chuī 吹 to blow

chūnjuǎn 春卷 spring rolls

chūntiān 春天 spring

chūzūchē 出租车 taxi

cì 次 time(s)

cóng 从 from

cóng … dào … 从 … 到 … from … to …

cónglái méiyǒu 从来没有 never

cōngmáng 匆忙 in a hurry, in a rush

cōngmíng 聪明 intelligent

cún 存:: to store up

D

dǎ chéng píngshǒu 打成平手 to tie the score

dǎ diànhuà 打电话 to make a phone call

dǎ gǔ 打鼓 to play drums

dǎ qiú 打球 to play ball

dǎ shígāo 打石膏 to have a plaster cast

dǎ zhēn 打针 to give/get an injection

dà 大 large, big

dǎ 打 to hit, to play (ball games with hands, bridge, and drums)

dā 搭 take (a form of transportation)

dàgài 大概 approximately, about

dàhào 大号 large (size)

dāi 待 (呆) to stay

dàlóu 大楼 building

dàngāo 蛋糕 cake

dǎng'àn 档案 file

dǎng'àn guì 档案柜 filing cabinet

dāngrán 当然 of course

dāo 刀 knife

dǎsuan 打算 to plan

dàtuǐ 大腿 thigh

dǎyìnjī 打印机 printer

dàxué 大学 university

dàyuē 大约 about

dǎzhé 打折 to give a discount

de 得 adverbial particle

de 的 adjectival particle, possessive particle

Déguó 德国 Germany

Déguórén 德国人 German (people)

Děng huìr jiàn! 等会见! See you later!

děng 等 to wait

Déwén 德文 German (language)

dì 第 prefix for ordinal numbers

diǎn cài 点菜 to order a dish

diǎn 点 to order (food); o'clock

diǎn zhōng 点钟 o'clock, hour

diànhuà 电话 telephone

diànhuàtíng 电话亭 telephone booth

diànnǎo 电脑 computer

diànshì 电视 television

diǎnxīn 点心 dim sum

diànyǐng 电影 film, movie

diànyǐngyuàn 电影院 cinema, movie theater

diàoyú 钓鱼 fishing

dìdi 弟弟 younger brother

dìtiě 地铁 subway

dìtiě zhàn 地铁站 subway station

dìzhǐ 地址 address

dōng 东 east

dōngtiān 冬天 winter

dōu 都 all

dù 度 degree (temperature)

Duìbùqǐ. 对不起。 Excuse me. (apologizing)

duìmiàn 对面 across the street

dùn 顿 measure word for meal

duōjiǔ 多久 how long?

duōshǎo 多少 how much

dùzi tòng 肚子痛 to have abdominal pain

dùzi 肚子 belly

E

è 饿 hungry

èr yuè 二月 February

èr 二 two

ěrduo 耳朵 ear

érqiě 而且 moreover, what's more …

èrshí 二十 twenty

érzi 儿子 son

étóu 额头 forehead

Éwén 俄文 Russian (language)

ěxin 恶心 to feel nauseous

F

fā chuánzhēn 发传真 to send a fax

fādǒu 发抖 to shiver

Fǎguó 法国 France

Fǎguórén 法国人 French (people)

fǎlǜ 法律 law

fàn hòu fú 饭后服 (medication) taken after a meal

fàn qián fú 饭前服 (medication) taken before a meal

fàn 饭 meal, food (lit., cooked rice)

fàndiàn 饭店 hotel

fàng 放 to put

fāngbiànmiàn 方便面 instant noodles

fàngjià 放假 on vacation, time off

fángjiān 房间 room

fànguǎn 饭馆 restaurant

fàngxué 放学 to finish class

fángzi 房子 house

fānqié 番茄 tomato

fàntīng 饭厅 dining room

fāshāo 发烧 to have a fever

Fǎwén 法文 French (language)

fāyán 发炎 inflammation

fēicháng 非常 very

fēijī 飞机 airplane

fēijī chǎng 飞机场 airport

fēn 分 minute

fēn 分 one one-hundredth of a yuán, equivalent to the cent; minute(s)

féngxiàn 缝线 to stitch up (a wound)

fěnhóngsè 粉红色 pink

fēnzhōng 分钟 minute(s)

fù xiànjīn 付现金 to pay in cash

fù 付 to pay

fùjìn 附近 nearby

fùqin 父亲 father
fùxí 复习 to review a lesson
fúzhuāng diàn 服装店 clothing store

G

gǎndào 感到 to feel
gāngcái 刚才 just now
gānjìng 干净 clean
gǎnlǎnqiú 橄榄球 football (American)
gǎnmào 感冒 a cold
gāo 高 tall
gè 个 measure word for people, cities, groups, and nations
gēge 哥哥 older brother
Gěi wǒ … 给我 bring me … , give me …
gěi 给 to bring, to give
gèng 更 even more
Gōng xǐ nǐ! 恭喜你! Congratulations!
gōngchē 公车 bus
gōngchē zhàn 公车站 bus stop
gōngchéng shī 工程师 engineer
gōngchéng 工程 engineering
gōngjīn 公斤 kilogram
gōngkè 功课 homework
gōnglǐ 公里 kilometers
gōngrén 工人 laborer, worker
gōngsī 公司 company
gōngyù 公寓 apartment
gōngyuán 公园 park
gōngzuò rényuán 工作人员 staff
gōngzuò 工作 work, job, profession
gōngzuòrì 工作日 weekday (lit., workday)
gǒu 狗 dog
guǎi ge wān 拐个弯 turn around the corner
guān 关 shut, close
guàn 罐 can (noun)
guāng 光 all gone
Guǎngdōngrén 广东人 Cantonese
gǔdiǎn yīnyuè 古典音乐 classical music
gūfu 姑夫 uncle (father's sister's husband)
gūgu 姑姑 aunt (father's sister)
guì 贵 expensive
guò mǎlù 过马路 to cross the street
guò 过 particle indicating completion of an action
guòlái 过来 to come over
guòshí 过时 out of style
guǒzhī 果汁 juice
gùyuán 雇员 employee

H

haí 还 still
háishì 还是 or (suggesting a preference)
háiyǒu 还有 also, in addition
hànshān 汗衫 T-shirt
hǎo ba 好吧 ok, alright, go ahead
… hǎo bù hǎo? … 好不好? … is it alright?
hǎo 好 good, fine, well
hǎochī 好吃 delicious
hē de 喝的 something to drink
hé 和 and
hē 喝 to drink
hé 盒 box, carton
hēi hújiāo 黑胡椒 black pepper
hēi 黑 black
hēisè 黑色 black
hěn duō cì 很多次 many times
hěn duō 很多 a lot, many, much
hěn jiǔ 很久 a long time
hěn, tǐng 很, 挺 very
hóng shāo zhūròu, hóng shāo ròu 红烧猪肉, 红烧肉 braised pork
hóng shāo 红烧 braised (in soy sauce)
hóng 红 red
hóngjiǔ 红酒 red wine
hónglùdēng 红绿灯 traffic light
hóngsè 红色 red
hòubiān 后边 behind
hòunián 后年 the year after next
hòutiān 后天 the day after tomorrow
huáxuě 滑雪 to ski
huài 坏 bad
huàn chē 换车 to change trains/subways/buses
huàn 换 to exchange
huǎnbùpǎo 缓步跑 jogging
huáng 黄 yellow
huángguā 黄瓜 cucumber
huángsè 黄色 yellow
huángyóu 黄油 butter
huàxué 化学 chemistry
huì 会 to know how to, will
huíguōròu 回锅肉 twice-cooked pork
huīsè 灰色 grey
Huítóu jiàn! 回头见! See you soon!
huìyì 会议 meeting
hújiāo 胡椒 pepper
húluóbo 胡萝卜 carrot

Essential Chinese

huǒchēzhàn 火车站 train station
huǒtuǐ 火腿 ham
huòzhě 或者 either … or …
hùshi 护士 nurse

J

jī 鸡 chicken
jǐ cì 几次 several times
jǐ ge 几个 several
jǐ tiān 几天 several days
jì xiàlái 记下来 to jot something down
jǐ 几 how many
jiā 家 family, home
jiābān 加班 to work overtime
jiákè 夹克 jacket
jiàn 件 measure word for garments worn over the upper part or full length of the body
jiàn 见 to see
Jiānádà 加拿大 Canada
jiānbǎng 肩膀 shoulder
jiǎnchá 检查 to examine, to check
jiǎng diànhuà 讲电话 on the phone
jiàngyóu 酱油 soy sauce
jiānzhí 兼职 part-time job
jiāo gōngkè 交功课 to submit homework
jiào 叫 to call, to be called
jiāo 教 to teach
jiǎo 脚 foot
jiǎo 角 one tenth of a yuán,
jiàoshì 教室 classroom
jiàotáng 教堂 church
jiàqī 假期 holiday, vacation
jiāyòng diànqì diàn 家用电器店 electronics store (lit., home appliances store)
jiāzhǎng 家长 parent
jīchǎng 机场 airport
jīdàn 鸡蛋 egg(s)
jǐdiǎn 几点 what time?, when?
jiē 街 street
jiémù 节目 program, show
jiějie 姐姐 older sister
jièmo 芥末 mustard
jièzhi 戒指 ring
jīguāng chàngpiàn 激光唱片 CD
jìjié 季节 season
jǐn 紧 tight
jìn 近 near
jǐngchá jú 警察局 police station

jǐngchá 警察 police officer
jīngcháng 经常 often, frequently
jìnlái 进来 come in
jīnnián 今年 this year
jīnsè 金色 gold
jīntiān wǎnshang 今天晚上 tonight
jīntiān xiàwǔ 今天下午 this afternoon
jīntiān zǎoshang 今天早上 this morning
jīntiān 今天 today
jīròu 鸡肉 chicken meat (boneless)
jiǔ yuè 九月 September
jiǔ 九 nine
jiù 旧 old (things)
jiǔ 酒 wine, alcoholic drink
jiùjiu 舅舅 uncle (mother's brother)
jiùmǔ/jiùmā 舅母, 舅妈 aunt (mother's brother's wife)
jiǔshí 九十 ninety
jízhōng jīngshén 集中精神 to concentrate
júsè 橘色 orange (color)
júzi 橘子 orange (fruit)

K

kāfēi 咖啡 coffee
kāichē 开车 to drive (a car)
kāihuì 开会 in a meeting, to have a meeting
kāimíng 开明 open-minded, enlightened
kāishǐ 开始 to start
kàn 看 to see, to look, to read
kàn diànyǐng 看电影 to go to a movie/the movies
kàn dìtú 看地图 to read a map
kàn qǐlái 看起来 appear(s) to be
kàn shū 看书 read a book
kàn xìjù 看戏剧 to see a play
kànjiàn 看见 to see
kǎo jī 烤鸡 roast chicken
kǎo 烤 roast
kǎo 考 to test
kǎoshì 考试 test, examination, to take an exam
kěnéng 可能 maybe, perhaps
kè 课 class
kè 刻 quarter of an hour
kē 棵 measure word for plants and grass
kē 颗 measure word for small plants and vegetables
kèběn 课本 textbook
kèqi 客气 polite
késou 咳嗽 cough

kètīng 客厅 living room
kèwài huódòng 课外活动 extracurricular activities
kěyǐ 可以 to be able (in terms of permission), to be allowed
kǒu 口 mouth; measure word for number of family members
kǔ 苦 bitter
Kuài … le 快　了 almost time to do something (lit. quickly … as of now)
kuài 块 colloquial word for yuán
kuài 快 fast, quick
kuàijìshī 会计师 accountant
kuàijì 会计 accounting
kuàilè 快乐 happy
kuàizi 筷子 chopsticks
kuǎnshì 款式 style
kùzi 裤子 pants

L

lā dùzi 拉肚子 to have diarrhea
lā xiǎotíqín 拉小提琴 to play violin
lā 拉 to pull
là 辣 hot, spicy
lái 来 to come
lánqiú 篮球 basketball
lán 蓝 blue
lánsè 蓝色 blue
lǎobǎn 老板 boss
Láojià. 劳驾。 Excuse me. (asking for a favor)
lǎoshī 老师 teacher
le 了 particle indicating that an action has been completed
lěng 冷 cold
lǐ 里 place, in
liǎn 脸 face
liáng tǐwēn 量体温 to take (someone's) temperature
liǎng 两 two (used to describe amount), measure word for cars, taxis, bicycles
liǎnjiá 脸颊 cheek
liànxí 练习 to practice
liányīqún 连衣裙 dress
lǐbài 礼拜 week
lǐbiān 里边 in, inside
lìjiāoqiáo 立交桥 overpass
líng 零 zero
língqián 零钱 change (monetary)

línjū 邻居 neighbor
lìshǐ 历史 history
liù yuè 六月 June
liù 六 six
liú 留 to stay, to keep
liúxiě 流血 to bleed
liúxíng yīnyuè 流行音乐 pop music
liúxíng 流行 popular, trendy
liúyán 留言 to leave a message
lǐyú 鲤鱼 carp
lóngxiā 龙虾 lobster
lǜ 绿 green
lù 路 road
lǚguǎn 旅馆 hotel
lùkǒu 路口 corner, intersection, block
lǜsè 绿色 green
lǜshī 律师 lawyer
lǚxíng 旅行 travel

M

ma 吗 question particle
máfan 麻烦 to trouble
　máfan nǐ 麻烦你 Could you…? (lit., bother you)
　Máfan nǐ gěi wǒmen … 麻烦你给我们 …
　　Could I trouble you for …
mǎi 买 to buy
màipiàn 麦片 cereal
Májiàng 麻将 Mahjong
mǎlíngshǔ 马铃薯 potatoes
māma 妈妈 mom
màn 慢 slow, slowly
mànpǎo 慢跑 jogging
māo 猫 cat
máo 毛 equivalent to the dime; colloquial word for jiǎo
máoyī 毛衣 sweater
màozi 帽子 hat
měi ge rén 每个人 everyone
Méi shì. 没事。 It's nothing., Don't worry., No problem.
měi tiān 每天 every day
měi 每 every, each
méiguì 玫瑰 rose
Měiguó 美国 America
Měiguórén 美国人 American (people)
mèimei 妹妹 younger sister
Méiyǒu wèntí. 没有问题。 No problem.
méiyǒu 没有 don't/doesn't have

ménkǒu 门口 in front of (lit. at the door)
mǐ 米 meters
miànbāo 面包 bread
miànshì 面试 interview
miàntiáo 面条 noodles
miǎo 秒 second(s)
míngbai 明白 to understand
míngnián 明年 next year
míngtiān 明天 tomorrow
mógu 蘑菇 mushrooms
mótuōchē 摩托车 motorcycle
mǔqīn 母亲 mother

N

nǎge zhàn 哪个站 which station
Nǎ guórén? 哪国人? What nationality?
nǎ tiān 哪天 which day
nàxiē 那些 those
nǎ 哪 which
ná 拿 to hold, to take
nà 那 that
nà … 那 … that, well … , in this/that case …
nǎichá 奶茶 milk tea
nǎinai 奶奶 grandmother (paternal side)
nàli 那里 there
nǎli 哪里 where, which place
nǎli yě 哪里也 anywhere
nán 南 south
nán 男 male
nán 难 difficult
nánhái 男孩 boy
nánháir 男孩儿 boy
Nánjīngrén 南京人 Nanjingese
nánrén 男人 man
nǎr yě 哪儿也 anywhere
nèikù 内裤 underpants
nèn 嫩 tender
néng(gòu) 能够 to be able (in terms of proficiency)
nǐ 你 you
nǐ de 你的 your, yours (singular)
nǐ hǎo 你好 hello
Nǐ hǎo ma? 你好吗? How are you?
Nǐ kěyǐ gěi wǒ … ma? 你可以给我 … 吗?
    May I have… ? (lit., Could you give me … ?)
Nǐ ne? 你呢? And you?
Nǐ yào…ma? 你要 … 吗? Do you want … ?
nián 年 year
niánqīng 年轻 young, youthful

nǐmen de 你们的 your, yours (plural)
Nǐmen yǒu … ma? 你们有 … 吗? Do you have
    … ?
nǐmen 你们 you (plural)
nín de 您的 your/yours (fml.)
niúnǎi 牛奶 milk
niúpái 牛排 steak
niúròu 牛肉 beef
nǚ 女 female
nǚ'ér 女儿 daughter
nǚháir 女孩儿 girl
nǚháizi 女孩子 girl
nǚhái 女孩 girl
nǚrén 女人 woman

P

pà 怕 to be scared of, to fear
pái dì yī míng 排第一名 to be placed first
páigǔ 排骨 spare ribs
páiqiú 排球 volleyball
pán 盘 measure word of general unit of ordering
    food; dish, plate
pángbiān 旁边 next to
pángtīng 旁听 to audit a class
pánzi 盘子 plate
pēngrèn 烹饪 cooking
péngyou 朋友 friend
piào 票 ticket
piàn 片 measure word for tile, tablets, other thin
    and flat objects; slice
piányi 便宜 inexpensive
piàoliang 漂亮 beautiful, pretty
pídài 皮带 belt
píjiǔ 啤酒 beer
píng 瓶 measure word for bottled drinks; bottle
píngguǒ 苹果 apple
pútao 葡萄 grape

Q

qī 七 seven
qī yuè 七月 July
qí zìxíngchē 骑自行车 cycling
qí 骑 to ride
qiǎn lǜsè 浅绿色 light green
qiǎn 浅 light
qián 钱 money
qiánbiān 前边 in front of
qiángzhuàng 强壮 strong

qiánnián 前年 the year before last
qiántiān 前天 the day before yesterday
qiáo 桥 bridge
qiǎokèlì 巧克力 chocolate
qìchē 汽车 car
qíncài 芹菜 celery
qǐng 请 please (used to make an invitation or ask a favor)
qǐng (shì)jià 请（事）假 to take personal leave
qǐng bìngjià 请病假 to take sick leave
Qǐng nǐ jiézhàng! 请你结帐! Check please!
qǐng nǐ/nín 请你/您 please ... (lit., please
   you ...), may I ...
qǐng wèn 请问 May I ask ... ?
Qǐng zài shuō yī cì. 请再说一次。 Please say
   that again.
qīng zhēng yú 清蒸鱼 steamed fish
qīng zhēng 清蒸 steamed
Qǐng zuò. 请坐。 Have a seat., Please sit.
qīnglǐ 清理 to clean, to tidy
qípáo 旗袍 traditional Chinese dress
qiú 球 ball
qiūtiān 秋天 autumn
qù 去 to go
qù hǎitān 去海滩 to go to the beach
qù tǐyùguǎn 去体育馆 to go to a stadium
qù yīyuàn 去医院 to go the hospital
qù zhěnsuǒ 去诊所 to go to a clinic
quánshēn 全身 whole body
qūgùnqiú 曲棍球 hockey
qùnián 去年 last year
qúnkù 裙裤 culottes, skort
qúnzi 裙子 skirt

R

ràng ... ba 让 ... 吧 let ...
ràng 让 to allow, to let
ràng wǒ 让我 let me
ránhòu 然后 after that, afterwards, then
rén 人 person, people
rènao 热闹 lively, busy, bustling
Rénmínbì 人民币 official Chinese currency
rènshi 认识 to know (someone), to meet
rénxíng dìdào 人行地道 underpass
rénxíngdào 人行道 sidewalk
Rìběn 日本 Japan
Rìběnrén 日本人 Japanese (people)
Rìwén 日文 Japanese (language)
ròu 肉 meat

rǔguǒ ... jiù 如果 ... 就 if ... (then)
rúguǒ 如果 if

S

sān yuè 三月 March
sān 三 three
sǎngzi tòng 嗓子痛 to have a sore throat
sǎngzi 嗓子 throat
sānshí 三十 thirty
sè 色 color
shāfā 沙发 sofa
shālā 沙拉 salad
shàngbān 上班 to go to work, to be at work
shàng chē 上车 to get on (a vehicle)
shàng dàxué 上大学 to attend university
shàng ge lǐbài 上个礼拜 last week
shàng ge yuè 上个月 last month
shàngxué 上学 to go to school, to attend school
shàngbiān, shàng 上边, 上 on (top of)
shāngdiàn 商店 shop/store
Shànghǎirén 上海人 Shanghaiese
shàngkè 上课 to attend (a) class, to go to class
shàngwǎng 上网 to go online
shāocài 烧菜 to cook
shāofàn 烧饭 to cook
sháozi 勺子 spoon
shéi 谁 who, whom
shēn 深 dark (colors)
shěng 省 to economize
shēnghuófèi 生活费 cost of living
shēngrì 生日 birthday
shēngwù 生物 biology
shénme dōngxi yě 什么东西也 anything
shénme rén yě, shéi yě 什么人也, 谁也 anyone
shénme shíhou 什么时候 what time, when
shénme 什么 what
shēnqǐng 申请 to apply
shěnshen 婶婶 aunt (father's younger
   brother's wife)
shétou 舌头 tongue
shī 诗 poetry
shí'er yuè 十二月 December
shíyī yuè 十一月 November
shí yuè 十月 October
shí 十 ten
shì 是 to be
shìchǎng 市场 market
shí'er 十二 twelve

Essential Chinese

shíhou 时候 time (in broad terms)
shíjiān 时间 time (in hour and minutes)
shímáo 时髦 fashionable, in style
shíwù 食物 food
shíyànshì 实验室 laboratory
shíyī 十一 eleven
shízhōng 时钟 clock
shízì lùkǒu 十字路口 intersection
shòuhuòyuán 售货员 store clerk
shǒu 手 hand
shǒubiǎo 手表 watch
shǒuwàn 手腕 wrist
shōuyīnjī 收音机 radio
shǒuzhǐ 手指 finger
shū 书 book
shuākǎ 刷卡 to pay by credit card
shuāng 双 pair
shūcài 蔬菜 vegetables
shūdiàn 书店 bookstore
shuì 睡 to sleep
shuìjiào 睡, 睡觉 to sleep
shuǐ 水 water
shuǐguǒ 水果 fruit
shūjià 书架 bookshelf
shuō 说 to say, to speak
shūshu 叔叔 uncle (father's younger brother)
shúxī 熟悉 to be familiar with
sì yuè 四月 April
sì 四 four
sìjìdòu 四季豆 string beans
sīrén bǔxí 私人补习 private tutoring
sìshí 四十 forty
suān 酸 sour
suàntóu 蒜头 garlic
sūdǎ shuǐ 苏打水 soda
suǒyǐ 所以 therefore

T

tā de 他的 his
tā de 她的 her (possessive pronoun), hers
tā 他 he, him
tā 她 she, her
tái 台 measure word for machines
tài 太 too
Tàijíquán 太极拳 Taiji / Tai Chi
tàitai 太太 Mrs., wife
tāmen de 他们的 their, theirs
tāmen 他们 they, them

tán gāngqín 弹钢琴 to play piano
tán 弹 to play (piano), to pluck
tāng 汤 soup
tàng 烫 hot, scalding
táng 糖 sugar, candy
tǎng 躺 to lie down
tāngchí 汤匙 spoon
tángdì 堂弟 cousin (father's brother's son, younger than you)
tánggē 堂哥 cousin (father's brother's son, older than you)
tángjiě 堂姐 cousin (father's brother's daughter, older than you)
tángmèi 堂妹 cousin (father's brother's daughter, younger than you)
tántan 谈谈 to have a chat, to discuss
tǐyù 体育 sports
tī zúqiú 踢足球 to play soccer
tī 踢 to kick
tiān 天 day
tián 甜 sweet
tiándiǎn 甜点 dessert
tiáo 条 measure word for garments worn over the lower half of the body, or for the objects that are long and thin, also for animals (dogs, fish, bulls...)
tiàowǔ 跳舞 to dance
tīng 听 to listen
tǐng 挺 quite, very
tīngdào 听到 to hear
tǐwēn 体温 temperature (body)
tíxǐng 提醒 to remind
tǐyù 体育 sport
tōngcháng 通常 usually
tóngshì 同事 colleague
tóngxué 同学 classmate
tóu tòng 头痛 to have a headache
tóuyūn 头晕 to feel dizzy
tǔdòu 土豆 potato
túhuà 图画 painting
tuǐ 腿 leg
tùle 吐了 to vomit
túshūguǎn 图书馆 library
túshūzhèng 图书证 library card
T-xùshān T-恤衫 T-shirt

W

wàibiān 外边 outside
wàigōng 外公 grandfather (maternal side)

wàiguó 外国 foreign

wàipó 外婆 grandmother (maternal side)

wàitào 外套 coat

wàiyǔ 外语 foreign language

wán de kāixīn 玩得开心 to have fun

wán yóuxì 玩游戏 to play a game

wǎn 碗 measure word for soup, rice; bowl

wǎn晚 evening

wǎncān 晚餐 dinner, supper

wǎng qián 往前 to go ahead

wǎng yòu zhuǎn 往右转 turn right

wǎng zuǒ zhuǎn 往左传 turn left

wàng 忘 to forget

wǎngqiú 网球 tennis

wǎnshang 晚上 evening, night

wàzi 袜子 socks

wèi tòng 胃痛 to have a stomachache

wèishēngjiān 卫生间 bathroom

wèishénme 为什么 why

wèn 问 to ask

wénjiàn 文件 document, file

wènlù 问路 to ask directions (lit., to ask the road)

wēnxí 温习 to review

wǒ bù xiǎng … 我不想 … I don't want to …

wǒ de 我的 my, mine

Wǒ xiǎng yào … 我想要 … I would like to have …

Wǒ yào … 我要 … I need …

wǒ 我 I, me

wòfáng 卧房 bedroom

wǒmen de 我们的 our, ours

wǒmen 我们 we, us

wǔ yuè 五月 May

wǔ 五 five

wǔcān 午餐 lunch

wùlǐ 物理 physics

X

xì 系 department (college level)

xī càn 西餐 western cuisine

xǐ 洗 to wash

xī 西 west

xiā 虾 shrimp

xià chē 下车 to get off (a vehicle)

Xià cì jiàn! 下次见! See you next time!

xià ge lǐbài 下个礼拜 next week

xià ge yuè 下个月 next month

xiàbiān, xià 下边, 下 under

xiān 先 first

xián 咸 salty

xiǎng 想 to want, think, would like …

xiàng 象 elephant

xiāngcǎo 香草 vanilla

Xiānggǎngrén 香港人 Hongkongese

xiāngjiāo 香蕉 banana

xiànjīn 现金 cash

xiānsheng 先生 Mr., husband

Xiànzài jǐdiǎn? 现在几点？ What time is it now?

xiànzài 现在 now

xiǎo zhèn 小镇 small town

xiǎo 小 small

xiǎojie 小姐 Miss., young lady

xiǎoshí 小时 hour (amount of time)

xiǎoshuō 小说 novel

xiǎotuǐ 小腿 calf

xiǎoxīn 小心 to be careful

xiāoyè 宵夜 late night snack

xiàoyuán 校园 campus

xiàozhǎng 校长 principal

xiàtiān 夏天 summer

xiàwǔ 下午 afternoon

Xībānyá 西班牙 Spain

Xībānyárén 西班牙人 Spanish (people)

Xībānyáwén西班牙文 Spanish (language)

Xièxie. 谢谢。 Thank you.

xiédiàn 鞋店 shoe store

xiézi 鞋子 shoes

xiězuò 写作 writing

xǐhuan 喜欢 to like

xīn 新 new

xīngqī èr 星期二 Tuesday

xīngqī liù 星期六 Saturday

xīngqī sān 星期三 Wednesday

xīngqī sì 星期四 Thursday

xīngqī tiān 星期天 Sunday

xīngqī wǔ 星期五 Friday

xīngqī yī 星期一 Monday

xīngqī 星期 week

xìng 姓 surname, to be called

xìngqù 兴趣 interest

xīnshuǐ 薪水 salary

xiōngbù tòng 胸部痛 to have chest pain

xiōngbù 胸部 chest

xiōngdìjiěmèi 兄弟姐妹 sibling

xǐshǒujiān 洗手间 restroom

xiūxi 休息 to rest

xìyuàn 戏院 theater
xué 学 to study, to learn
xuésheng 学生 student
xuéxiào 学校 school
xuēzi 靴子 boots

Y

yā 鸭 duck
yáchǐ 牙齿 tooth
yángcōng 洋葱 onion
yǎnjing 眼睛 eye
yánjiūshēng 研究生 graduate student
yánsè 颜色 color
yánjiūyuàn, yánjiūsuǒ 研究院, 研究所 graduate school
yàofáng 药房 pharmacy
yào 要 to want
yě 也 also
yèxiāo 夜宵 late night snack
yéye 爷爷 grandfather (paternal side)
yībǎiwàn 一百万 one million
yībǎi 一百 one hundred
yī bēi jiǔ 一杯酒 a glass of wine
yī dǎ 一打 one dozen
yī diǎndiǎn 一点点 a few/a little
yī huìr 一会儿 a while
yīqiān 一千 one thousand
yīwàn 一万 ten thousand
yī yuè 一月 January
yī 一 one
Yìdàlì 意大利 Italy
Yìdàlìrén 意大利人 Italian (people)
Yìdàlìwén 意大利文 Italian (language)
yífu 姨夫 uncle (mother's sister's husband)
yīfu 衣服 clothes, clothing
yímǔ/yímā 姨母/姨妈 aunt (mother's sister)
yìnbiǎojī 印表机 printer
yīnggāi 应该 should, ought to
Yīngguó 英国 Britain
Yīngguórén 英国人 British (people)
Yīngwén 英文 English (language)
yínháng 银行 bank
yínsè 银色 silver
yīnwèi 因为 because
yīnyuè 音乐 music
yīqǐ 一起 together
yīqián 以前 ago
yīqiè 一切 everything

yīshēng 医生 doctor
yīxiē 一些 some
yīyàng 一样 same
yīyuàn 医院 hospital
yīzhí wǎng qián zǒu 一直往前走 go straight ahead
yīzhí 一直 straight
yǐzi 椅子 chair
yòng zhīpiào fùqián 用支票付钱 to pay by check
yōngjǐ 拥挤 crowded
yǒu duō yuǎn? 有多远？ how far?
yǒu rén 有人 someone
yóuyǒng 游泳 to swim
yòu 右 right
yǒu 有 to have, there is/are
yòu … yòu … 又 … 又 … and (for connecting two adjectives or adverbs)
yǒu … nàme 有 … 那么 as … adjective/adverb as … (used for people and things far away)
yǒu … zhème 有 … 这么 as … adjective/adverb as … (used for people and things nearby)
… yǒu méiyǒu … ? … 有没有 … ？ Do (you) have … ?
yòubiān 右边 the right side of
yóujú 邮局 post office
yú 鱼 fish
yuán 元 currency unit, equivalent to the dollar unit
yuǎn 远 far
yuángōng 员工 staff
yuǎnzú 远足 hiking
yuè lái yuè 越来越 more and more, less and less
yuè 月 month
yuē 约 to make an appointment, to make a date
yújiā 瑜伽 yoga
yǔmáoqiú 羽毛球 badminton
yùndòngxié 运动鞋 sneakers
yùxí 预习 to prepare for a lesson
yǔyī 雨衣 raincoat
yùyuē 预约 to make an appointment

Z

zài … hé … zhōngjiān 在 … 和 … 中间 between … and …
Zài gěi wǒ … 再给我 … Give me another …
zài jiā 在家 at home
Zàijiàn. 再见。 Goodbye.
zài lái … 再来 … one more, another
zài lái yīdiǎn … 再来一点 … a little more of …

zài lùkǒu 在路口 on the corner

zài nàli 在那里 over there

zài nǎli? 在哪里? (At) where? Where is … ?

zài nǎli? 在哪里? Where is … ?

zài 再 again

zài 在 at, in, on; particle indicating an ongoing action, to be (located) at

zāng 脏 dirty

zǎocān 早餐 breakfast

zǎoshang 早上 morning

zěnme yàng? 怎么样 how … ?

zěnme zǒu 怎么走 how to get to … ?

zěnyàng 怎样 what, how

zhàn 站 to stand

zhāng 张 measure word for objects that have a flat surface (tables, desks, chairs…)

zhāngkāi 张开 to open (the mouth)

zhǎo 找 to look for, to find

zháoliáng 着凉 to catch a cold

zhàopiàn 照片 photograph

zhàoxiàngjī 照相机 camera

zhèbiān 这边 this way

zhège lǐbài 这个礼拜 this week

zhège yuè 这个月 this month

zhèxiē 这些 these

zhe 着 particle indicating an ongoing state of being

zhè 这 this

zhèlǐ 这里 here

zhéxué 哲学 philosophy

zhī 只 measure word for objects that are pointed and thin, utensils, and some animals

zhǐ 纸 paper

zhīdào 知道 to know a fact, to know something

zhīhòu 之后 after

zhǐjia 指甲 fingernail

zhīpiào 支票 check (payment)

zhīqián 之前 before

zhǐshì 只是 it's only …

zhǒng 种 kind (noun)

Zhōngcài 中菜 Chinese cuisine

Zhōngguó 中国 China

Zhōngguórén 中国人 Chinese (people)

zhōnghào 中号 medium (size)

zhōngjiān 中间 between

zhōngtóu 钟头 hour (amount of time)

Zhōngwén 中文 Chinese (language)

zhōngwǔ 中午 noon

zhōngyú 终于 finally

zhǒu 肘 elbow

zhōumò 周末 weekend

zhù zài 住在 to live in

zhuānyè, zhǔxiū 专业, 主修 major

zhǔnbèi 准备 to prepare

zhǔnshí 准时 on time

zhuōzi 桌子 table

zhūpái 猪排 pork chop(s)

zhūròu 猪肉 pork

zìdiǎn 字典 dictionary

zìjǐ 自己 self

zǐsè 紫色 purple

zìxíngchē 自行车 bicycle

zōngsè 棕色 brown

zǒngshì 总是 always

Zǒu ba. 走吧。 Leave. (polite)

zǒulù 走路 on foot

zǒu 走 to leave, to walk

zǒu 走 to leave, to get out

zúgēn 足跟 heel

zuì hǎo de 最好的 the best

zuì 最 the most

zuǐba 嘴巴 mouth

zuǐchún 嘴唇 lips

zuìhòu qīxiàn 最后期限 deadline

zuò xīndiàntú 做心电图 to take a cardiogram

zuò yùndòng 做运动 to play a sport

zuò 做 to do, to make

zuò 坐 sit, to take (a form of transportation)

zuǒ 左 left

zuǒbiān 左边 the left side of

zuòfàn 做饭 to cook

zuótiān 昨天 yesterday

zuǒyòu 左右 around

zúqiú 足球 soccer (football)